DOCUMENTS OF MODERN HISTORY

General Editor:

A. G. Dickens

The Middle East, 1914 – 1979

T. G. Fraser

EDWARD ARNOLD

Copyright © T. G. Fraser 1980

First published 1980 by
Edward Arnold (Publishers) Ltd
41 Bedford Square, London WC1B 3DQ

British Library Cataloguing in Publication Data

The Middle East, 1914 – 1979. — Documents of modern history).
  1. Near East — History — 20th century — Sources
  I. Fraser, Thomas Grant
  956'.008   DS62.4

ISBN 0-7131-6292-9 Pbk

Printed and bound in Great Britain at
The Camelot Press Ltd, Southampton

Abbreviations

CAB	British Cabinet Conclusions
Cmd	British Parliamentary (Command) Paper
DBFP	*Documents on British Foreign Policy*
DSB	United States *Department of State Bulletin*
FRUS	*Foreign Relations of the United States*
GAOR	General Assembly Official Records
OAPEC	Organization of Arab Petroleum Exporting Countries
OPEC	Organization of the Petroleum Exporting Countries
PGI	Provisional Government of Israel
PLO	Palestine Liberation Organization
SCOR	Security Council Official Records
SWB	*Summary of World Broadcasts*
UAR	United Arab Republic
UNEF	United Nations Emergency Force
UNO	United Nations Organization
UNRWA	United Nations Relief and Works Agency for Palestine Refugees in the Near East
UNSCOP	United Nations Special Committee on Palestine

Contents

Acknowledgements

The publisher wishes to thank the following for permission to reproduce copyright material:

BBC Monitoring Service for Summary of World Broadcasts; the State Information Service of Egypt for the Treaty of Peace between the Arab Republic of Egypt and Israel; the State Information Service of Israel for the Declaration of the Establishment of the State of Israel; Europa Publications Ltd for the Palestinian National Charter from *The Middle East and North Africa*; Her Majesty's Stationery Office for British Parliamentary (Command) Papers, British Cabinet Conclusions and Documents on British Foreign Policy; *Palestine* for PLO Information Bulletin and United Nations for General Assembly Official Records and Security Council Official Records.

Preface

In preparing this book, I have incurred numerous debts which I gladly acknowledge. It could never have been completed without the generous financial assistance of the British Academy and the New University of Ulster, which enabled me to work in London, New York and Vienna. I am grateful to the staffs of the following libraries and repositories for their hospitality and courteous assistance: Chatham House Library and the Public Record Office, London; the BBC Archives, Caversham Park, Reading; the New University of Ulster Library, Coleraine; the OPEC Library, Vienna; the Dag Hammarskjöld Library, United Nations Headquarters, New York, and the Library of the Council on Foreign Relations, Inc., New York. I acknowledge the permission of HM Stationery Office and of the BBC Monitoring Service to reproduce material, and the co-operation of the US Government Printing Office and of the information services of Egypt and Israel. The following helped me with their intimate knowledge of British Middle Eastern policy: Sir Francis Evans, Minister and Ambassador to Israel, 1951 – 54; Sir John Martin, Secretary to the Peel Commission, 1936 – 37, Principal Private Secretary to (Sir) Winston Churchill, 1941 – 45, and a member of the British delegation to the UN, 1947; and the late Professor L.F. Rushbrook Williams, Adviser Middle East Affairs, Ministry of Information. I am always glad to recall my debts to Dr I.H. Nish and Professor W.V. Wallace, who fostered my interest in modern international history. Naturally, I assume sole responsibility for the interpretations presented in this book. Its appearance would never have been possible without the unstinting forbearance of my most sensitive critic, my wife Grace, and our children who had to take the strain of my various absences.

Castlerock,
Northern Ireland.

January 1980

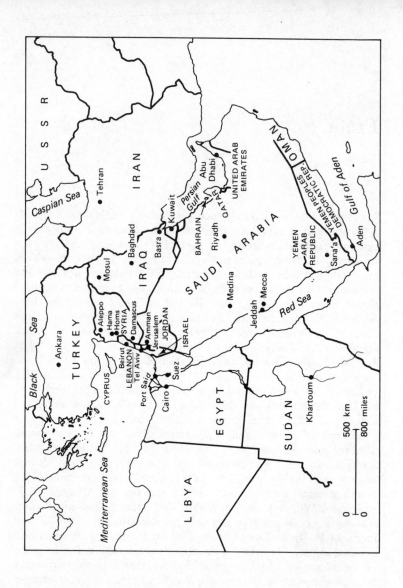

Map 1:   General Political Map of the Middle East in 1979

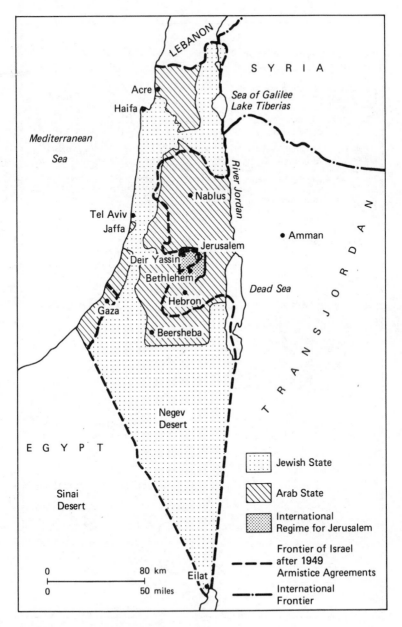

Map 2:   UN Partition Plan

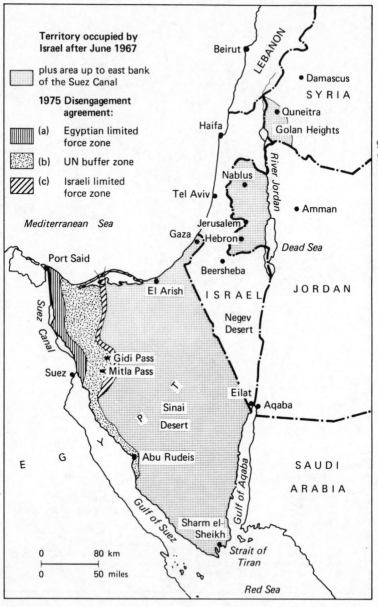

Map 3: Arab-Israeli relations after 1967

Introduction

This book attempts to document the twentieth-century transformation of the Middle East from a region of the world dominated by the centuries-old rule of the Ottoman Turks or the more recent imperialism of Europe into an area of absorbing interest for the modern historian. It can, of course, be said that all history is interesting, and it is undeniable that the Middle East, with its unique contributions to the development of civilization, religion and science, should always have retained an important place in human understanding. But from the early sixteenth century, when its ancient culture was subsumed by the martial but philistine Ottomans and the expansion of Atlantic civilization led to the decay of its trade routes, it entered into a long period of decline and neglect.

In many respects 1914 is an unrealistic date with which to begin an examination of its modern development. Arab nationalism dates back at least to the early 1880s, with the emergence in Beirut of a small group of intellectuals anxious to break free from Ottoman rule and Colonel Arabi's unsuccessful campaign in 1881-1882 to prevent British control of Egypt. Zionism, too, found serious expression at this time. In Russia, the anti-semitic pogroms which followed the assassination of Tsar Alexander II in 1881 and continued into the twentieth century, drove hundreds of thousands of a gravely embattled Jewish community to migrate from the empire, others into ideas of social revolution, or, for a determined minority, into an assertion of their own nationalism through settlement in Turkish-ruled Palestine. In the increasingly anti-Jewish atmosphere of *fin de siècle* Vienna, the Austrian journalist Theodor Herzl articulated the pessimism felt by many Jews with the publication in 1896 of his seminal pamphlet *Der Judenstaat* (*The Jewish State*), and helped give Zionism formal expression with the organization of its first congress at Basle the following year. If the First World War saw Ottoman rule in the Middle East replaced by an Anglo-French hegemony, the forces of Arab nationalism and Zionism which were to render this ephemeral were already well under way.

The events of 1914-1918 not only accelerated the development of the two movements to positions scarcely imaginable only a few years before; they saw the intensification of that great power interest in the Middle East which was to be a complicating factor in its evolution throughout the entire period. During the war many marriages of convenience were cobbled together to exert diplomatic pressure or serve the ends of strategy. With Turkey's entry into the war, the Middle East became an area of real concern for Britain, albeit of a less pressing nature than her European preoccupations. While some British officers in the area felt a romantic sympathy with national aspirations, the overriding motives behind the diplomatic manoeuvres (1) which induced an army of Arab irregulars to fight against the Turks were the military and strategic ones which inevitably govern policy in wartime. Not all Arabs followed the lead of Britain's Hashemite allies, many preferring to fight beside the Turks for the integrity of *dar al-Islam* ('the domain of Islam'). Nonetheless, the pledges Britain made and the collapse of Ottoman power in the Levant before the forces of General Allenby and the Hashemites gave new excitement and verve to Arab political aspirations. If the 'independence of the Arabs' which had seemingly been promised fell short of total realization, violent protests in the immediate post-war years, notably in Iraq and Egypt, forced important British concessions which saved the Arab world from becoming a mere accretion to the Empire.

To a greater extent than with the pledges to the Arabs, the Balfour declaration in favour of a Jewish national home in Palestine combined the positive commitment of some members of the British government with wartime calculation (5). The active canvassing of the Zionist concept in political circles before and during the war by Chaim Weizmann and his associates in the British branch of the movement had engaged the sympathy of the Foreign Secretary, Arthur Balfour, and Prime Minister David Lloyd George, though the chief reasons for making the declaration are to be found in the hopes of using it to influence American and Russian Jews at a time when allied war prospects were bleak (4). Cabinet hesitations about sanctioning the proposal centred around Edwin Montagu's anxiety about its implications for assimilated Jews like himself and Lord Curzon's concern for the established Arab population (3). The form of the declaration reflected an inevitable compromise between the two sets of views (4). Although the resulting commitment was less explicit than Weizmann had hoped, it was welcomed by the Zionists and came to be written into the terms of the League of Nations mandate which Britain assumed in 1922. Her period of Middle Eastern dominance did not prove to be a happy one. Faced throughout the region with an Arab nationalism she had helped to nurture, her Palestine policy was fated to lurch uncertainly from one expedient to another, perhaps the natural result of the ambiguities in her wartime policies.

But great power involvement in the Middle East was not confined to Britain; events in Germany, too, had the profoundest implications for Palestine. Zionism had always contained elements who saw it as the positive affirmation of the Jews' right to self-expression as a people, but to others it was something less optimistic, the necessary relief of the *Judennot*, the need to find sanctuary from persecution. With Adolf Hitler's assumption of power in Germany this latter aspect came to the fore. From 1933 until almost the outbreak of war, the Jewish population of Palestine increased dramatically as refugees fleeing actual and potential persecution in Europe settled in the country. The immigration of nearly 150,000 in the first three years of Nazi rule gave the National Home the prospect of viability, but, with Jews now numbering almost a third of the Arab total, it also prompted the latter into a strenuous effort to defend their identity. The Arab rising, which began in April 1936 and lasted almost three years, while failing to end British rule, was nevertheless of the greatest significance. The persistence with which the Palestinians maintained their struggle in the teeth of a strong British garrison excited admiration throughout the Middle East, making their cause the emblem of Arab nationalism. Palestine assumed a place in the Arab imagination which it never entirely lost, feelings which Britain had to acknowledge in 1939 in her attempt to reach a solution. This was also the period when partition, the solution adopted by the United Nations a decade later, was first proposed by the Peel Commission in 1937, on the grounds that the two parties to the dispute were devoid of any sense of common loyalty (9). Two years later, however, under pressure in Europe and the Middle East, Britain renounced any commitment to the creation of a Jewish state in Palestine (10), and the Arabs had seemingly assured their position.

With hindsight, it is clear that this was not so. By 1945, the international influences bearing upon the Middle East had changed dramatically. The appalling fate of European Jewry at the hands of the Nazis (11, 12) made the Zionists grimly determined that the

battered survivors would find a secure refuge and that the establishment of a state would guarantee their people against any such future
calamity. Alienated by the 1939 White Paper policy (10), the official
Jewish Agency, led by David Ben-Gurion, and its underground army,
the Haganah, devoted its energies to a well orchestrated international
campaign to end the British mandate, generally harrassing the work
of the mandatory government, and organizing illegal immigration
from the European refugee camps (19). This breach in relations
between the mandatory power and mainstream Zionism was more
than matched by the actions of the avowedly violent Irgun Zvai Leumi
('National Military Organization'), the heirs of Vladimir Jabotinsky's
pre-war Revisionists who had never shared the Jewish Agency's faith in
cooperation with the British. Directed by Menachem Begin, the Irgun
waged a ruthless underground war against the British (16, 19). Zionist
pressure found active support in the United States, which had
emerged from the war with unparalled wealth and influence. While
some members of the State Department, mindful of the importance of
the Arab world and its oil, took a broad view of American interests in
the Middle East (23), the Democratic administration of Harry S.
Truman became firmly wedded to support of the Zionists, partly for
domestic political reasons and partly out of a sense of shock over what
had happened under Hitler. The combined pressure proved too much
for an economically enfeebled Britain, increasingly unable to sustain
even the simulacrum of its imperial position in the Middle East (14).
When attempts to solve the problem in conjunction with the United
States (13, 14, 15) or through agreement between Jew and Arab (17,
18) only served to emphasize the problem's intractability, the British
government, embittered at having to shoulder alone the burden of
Palestine, referred the issue to the United Nations (18).

Two general observations ought to made about the nature of the
United Nations at this time. Palestine was the first major international
issue which the new organization had to consider; as such, members
were anxious that its future would be approached in a responsible
manner which would demonstrate that the United Nations was not a
re-creation of its disgraced and ineffectual inter-war predecessor.
Secondly, it was still a quite compact body of some fifty-five members,
within which the United States and the Soviet Union, each committed
to support for a Jewish state (30), wielded powerful influence. The
United Nations addressed the problem with conspicuous thorough-
ness. In its five-volume report, the United Nations Special Committee
on Palestine (UNSCOP) advocated partition for much the same

reasons as the British Peel Commission ten years before (**21, 9**). Although the details of the partition scheme gave the Zionists much less than they had wished, they accepted it (**25**), but the Palestinians held to their total opposition (**24**), as did their Arab allies (**29**). The partition proposals were highly complex, involving the establishment of two mutually suspicious states, an international regime for Jerusalem and an economic union (**26, 28, Map 2**). Given Arab determination to frustrate the whole idea, perhaps it was never realistic; certainly, any hope of success rested entirely upon the operation of a clear-cut and generally acceptable machinery of implementation, which in the event proved lacking. Britain had repeatedly made plain her resolve to do nothing to implement the proposal (**27**). True to her word, she refused to allow the United Nations Palestine Commission, itself denied armed assistance by the Security Council, to set up the complicated structures envisaged in the partition scheme (**33**). The collapse of United Nations authority before this dying kick of the mandatory promised ill for the organization's future and in the absence of any firm guidance violence became the characteristic feature of Palestinian life as each side tried to gain the maximum advantage before the British departure.

The termination of British mandatory rule and the war which immediately followed marked a decisive period in modern Middle Eastern history. The foundation of the State of Israel (**35**) brought into existence a distinctive political entity which gave an enhanced sense of pride and nationhood to Jews throughout the world, but which was generally regarded in the Middle East as negating the national aspirations of the Palestinian Arabs. The first Middle Eastern war (**36, 37**), unsuccessfully waged on their behalf by the armies of the neighbouring Arab states, brought the Palestinians nothing but ruin. By February 1949, the basic pattern of future Middle Eastern affairs had been set. In the fighting the Israelis successfully defended their new state's existence and advanced its frontiers in several important respects (**Map 2**). Despite the economic and political uncertainties which were to beset them in the early 1950s, the Israelis had gained sufficient time and territory to consolidate their state, settling thousands of Jews from the European camps and the Middle East. For the Arab countries defeat stimulated political discontent, while for the Palestinians it inaugurated the frustrations of exile and the despair of stifled ambition. Amid the war the Palestinians had become the dispossessed of the Middle East (**41**).

Arab nationalism, which had found its symbol in Palestine, reached its modern maturity with the revolution which broke out in Egypt in 1952 (**42**) and culminated in the establishment of Gamal Abdul Nasser as head of state two years later. Nasser's aims of economic improvement for his people and the end of Britain's presence on the Suez canal were complicated by the fact that the defeats of 1948-1949 still rankled with the Arab army officers of his generation. His success in negotiating British evacuation of the canal zone in 1954 revealed him as a figure to be reckoned with in the Arab world, while his arms agreement with the Soviet Union the following year (**44**) demonstrated his desire to assert a new flexibility in diplomacy, even if it displeased the Americans who had patronized him during his rise to power.

Yet his policies were attracting powerful enemies. In 1955 and early 1956, his actions over the British-sponsored Baghdad Pact, the Algerian war and Palestinian guerrilla action from Sinai earned him growing hostility in London, Paris and Jerusalem, and the suspicion of the United States. The Middle Eastern crisis of 1956 grew out of the American decision to withdraw their offer of financial support for the Aswan High Dam (**45**), with which Britain readily concurred. The tension which built up over Nasser's retaliatory nationalization of the Suez Canal Company exposed the deep resentment felt by many in the West at the growth of Arab nationalism. Hopelessly muddled as to whether their aim was to 'internationalize' the canal, overthrow Nasser, or both, the British and French governments embarked on the preparation of a military expedition. Anxious to strike at the nascent force of Nasserism, the Israeli government of David Ben-Gurion agreed with the French that an attack by them in Sinai might serve as the justification for intervention on the canal, a proposal which was to be sanctioned by a rather shamefaced British government. The consequent diplomatic debacle which was inflicted upon the British and French after their landing at Port Said is generally accepted as a watershed in post-war history. It starkly emphasized the weakness of Western Europe, especially in relation to post-imperial military action. In contrast, by her crucial financial pressure on London to cease hostilities and her subsequent success in forcing a reluctant Israel to withdraw from Sinai, the United States showed that she was now a Middle Eastern factor of the first importance. Association with the western powers had been an unhappy experience for Israel. Universal condemnation of the Anglo-French action obscured the nature of her military victory in Sinai, while American pressure on her after the war was keenly resented. In tangible terms, she gained freedom of navigation through the Gulf of Aqaba (**53, 54**), but for the

Israelis the real lessons of 1956 lay in freedom from inhibiting entanglements and the value of military preparedness. As the result of the Suez affair, Nasser attained a pinnacle of popularity unequalled by any Arab of recent history. Inspired by the desire to guide a strong pan-Arab bloc in world affairs, for a time he seemed to act out of unerring instinct in foreign policy. Perhaps his year of greatest triumph was 1958 when his enemies, the Iraqi Hashemites, were overthrown and Syria joined him in forming the United Arab Republic.

But the concept of Arab unity proved elusive. The republican regime in Iraq proved to be no more attracted by Nasser than its Hashemite predecessor and by 1961 Egypt's union with Syria had dissolved amid mutual recrimination. From that time, even though his personal standing in the Arab world remained impressive, he seemed inexorably to lose the initiative in its affairs. Other states, notably Syria, took up the issue of Palestine, which slowly reasserted its old place at the centre of Arab preoccupations. The Cairo conference of 1964, which resulted in the formation of the Palestine Liberation Organization (PLO), was at least in part an attempt by Nasser to retain a decisive voice in events (55). From 1962, too, a large proportion of his army became enmeshed in an expensive but apparent fruitless commitment to the republican regime in the Yemen against royalist tribesmen supported from Saudi Arabia. By 1967, he no longer seemed to be the master of events. The initiative in taking action against Israel had fallen to Syria and sections of the Palestinians over whom he had little influence (56). Their joint harrassment led even the moderate Israeli government of Levi Eshkol into retaliation, the brunt of which seemed to fall upon Jordan.

When warnings of an impending Israeli attack upon Syria came to him on what seemed good authority in May 1967, Nasser felt that he had no alternative but to react (57, 58). If at first his former sureness of touch in foreign affairs seemed to have returned when the United Nations complied with his demand for the removal of their troops from Sinai, events then began to develop along a direction which proved disastrous for his cause. His blockade of the Straits of Tiran (58, 60) seemingly took little account of the reactions of an Israeli government which was itself being subjected to mounting pressure over what was considered to be its supine attitude in the face of Arab provocations during the previous two years, but which did not disguise its deep concern with this particular issue (59). As the declared aims of Nasser's confrontation with Israel became more ambitious (61), its success would inevitably depend on his armed forces, whose efficiency under his old friend Field-Marshal Amer had deteriorated badly. The result was a war in which Egypt, Jordan and Syria lost extensive territory, armaments, troops and prestige before a brilliantly executed Israeli attack.

In its consequences for the Middle East the 1967 war proved perhaps to be of even greater significance than 1956. Security Council Resolution 242 (**67**) and the Jarring mission which sought to implement it (**74**) indicated a widespread recognition that the region's tensions should move towards a solution acceptable in the international community. The two great powers became increasingly drawn into the situation. The Soviet Union worked hard to re-create the shattered Egyptian army through the supply of military hardwear and the cooperation of personnel, creating an apparent dependence which both President Nasser and his successor, Anwar al-Sadat, found irksome. The United States, perhaps alarmed by suspicions that Israel had developed a nuclear capacity, became prominent in diplomacy (**64, 72, 73**). But United Nations and American efforts proved unavailing against the hardened public positions of the chief protagonists (**68, 69**). In the aftermath of their defeat, the Arab states had few diplomatic counters to move, except recognition of Israel and the withholding of direct negotiations with her. While the resolutions of the Khartoum summit seemed to promise nothing but intransigence on these issues (**66**), acceptance of Resolution 242 implied a willingness to recognize Israel's 'sovereignty, territorial integrity and political independence'. Despite the awesome financial burden of her military commitments, Israel felt few inducements to make concessions, especially as most Israelis believed that their state's existence had been questioned in May-June 1967 and that their subsequent military dominance in the region guaranteed its future for a long time to come. Most Israelis were relieved that the new frontiers they had gained (**Map 3**) gave the appearance of greater military security, while many saw the occupation of the West Bank as the opportunity to expand into territories they viewed as part of the historic land of Israel. This was an issue which Israeli governments had to approach with caution. In July 1967, the United Nations General Assembly voted to condemn Israel's annexation of east Jerusalem by ninety-nine votes to none, with twenty abstentions (**65**). Moreover, military occupation of the West Bank involved Israel with a large Palestinian population at a time when the PLO was evolving from a vociferous but ineffectual body into an aggressive and increasingly sophisticated defender of the Arab position. Although their methods were often brutal, the violence waged inside Israel and abroad by the two principal guerrilla groups, Fatah and the Popular Front for the Liberation of Palestine, ensured that the world was continually reminded of a 'Palestinian dimension' to the Middle East. By 1974, the PLO had secured for itself a key position in Middle Eastern affairs, a fact which steadily gained international acceptance (**80, 81, 83**), even if it remained totally beyond the pale as far as the Israelis were concerned (**82**).

The previous year had been one of notable success for the Arabs. Even if it had ended in something of a military stalemate, the October 1973 war put fresh heart into the Arab world (**78**). It was not simply that in the fighting against a hard-pressed but brave and resourceful Israeli army the Egyptians and Syrians confounded those who had denigrated their courage and technical proficiency; the crisis revealed that oil had transformed the Arab world's international importance. Although oil was used in the war as an overtly political device (**99, 100**), its new importance was due at least as much to economic forces. Oil was the one great resource possessed by the Middle Eastern exporting countries. For some time, they had been building up their position to ensure the most favourable pricing structure and that future production would be regulated in accordance with their own needs, not those of the consuming countries (**95, 96, 97, 98, 101, 102**). As well as bringing dramatic improvements in their economic position, success in achieving these aims brought Saudi Arabia and the other oil exporting countries of the Middle East powerful diplomatic influence (**85**)

By 1974, intensive negotiations were under way to try to settle the region's outstanding issues. While at various stages most Middle Eastern countries, as well as the Soviet Union, became involved in this process in some capacity, in the end the most significant results proved to be bilateral agreements between Egypt and Israel with the United States acting as agent between them. The Sinai agreement of 1975 (**84**) was as important for the barriers of suspicion it helped remove as for the concessions each side made. Any evaluation of the 'peace process' initiated by President Sadat's visit to Israel two years later must still be tentative. If its author believed that his unprecedented gesture and his Knesset speech (**87**) would cut the Gordian knot of the tangled negotiations by altering the psychological approach of the Israelis, then to a degree he succeeded. The government of Menachem Begin ultimately responded by retreating from some long-cherished positions, but equally there can be little doubt that the procrastinating nature of its negotiating techniques soured to a considerable extent the early feelings of good will. The 'Framework for the Conclusion of a Peace Between Egypt and Israel' (90), negotiated at Camp David in September 1978, and the actual peace treaty signed the following March (93) gave Israel her ambition of a bilateral treaty with her most powerful antagonist, at the cost of surrendering all her military and civilian positions in Sinai and promising to negotiate on the future of the West Bank. The treaty not only gave Egypt the return of her territory but the prospect of concentrating in future on her economic development rather than armed confrontation. Sensitive to the charge that she had asserted Nile valley nationalism to the detriment of wider Arab issues (92) Egypt could point to the 'Framework for Peace in the Middle East agreed at Camp David' (91) as the gauge of her adherence to her original pledge to negotiate for a comprehensive peace settlement which would include a solution acceptable to the Palestinians. It was a daunting prospect for all likely to be concerned.

I
Britain and the Palestine Mandate, 1914 – 1945

At the beginning of the First World War, many Egyptians chafed resentfully at the continuing British presence in their country, but Arabs in the Turkish empire centred their hopes for national independence on the expulsion of their Ottoman rulers. Faced with the necessity to sustain a war against Turkey, while undertaking a campaign of unprecedented dimensions in Europe, Britain found it expedient to bid for the support of some of these Arab groups. It is in this context that her pledges for the support of Arab independence contained in the correspondence between Sir Henry McMahon, High Commissioner in Egypt, and the Hashemite Husein, Sherif of Mecca, must be seen (1). The Balfour declaration, issued to the Zionists in November 1917, is more complex, with British cabinet reactions ranging from warm conviction on the part of Arthur Balfour, through Lord Curzon's grudging acceptance to Edwin Montagu's anguished opposition. The mixture of motives which gave rise to a document of historic significance but peculiar vulnerability to conflicting interpretation can be seen in the discussions which produced it (2, 3, 4, 5). Documents 6 and 7 show that the contradictions were present from the beginning of Britain's unhappy association with Palestine, the mandate for which was formally awarded her by the League of Nations in 1922. By that date, Arab opposition to Zionist endeavours had become so apparent that in the Churchill White Paper (8) Britain advanced a definition of the Balfour declaration which moved far from what its signatory at least had anticipated. In the early 1930s, the rise of German Nazism and anti-semitism elsewhere in Europe made Palestine an increasingly attractive prospect for Jews, since 1924 largely denied their traditional refuge in the United States. Their arrival in large numbers provoked the Arab rebellion of 1936. Britain's response, the Peel Commission of 1936 – 1937, is of considerable significance, because, under the forceful inspiration of Professor Reginald Coupland, it concluded that partition was the only possible solution for Palestine (**9**). Reluctant acceptance of this by the Jews and the outraged hostility of the Arabs presaged what was to happen ten years later, but the unfavourable response of the Woodhead Commission the following year put the concept into apparent limbo. With the approach of war in 1939, expediency once again governed Britain's Middle Eastern policy. The necessity of appeasing the Arabs and ensuring essential oil supplies led to the White Paper of 1939 which outlined Palestine's ultimate independence as a largely Arab state (**10**). The restrictions it put on Jewish immigration at a time when the Nazis were about to embark on their policy of extermination led to such bitter resentment that even before the war's end Zionist acts of violence broke out against British mandatory rule. Documents **11** and **12** briefly indicate the nature of the Jews' fate under Nazism. The virtual extermination of European Jewry forms the essential background to Zionist intransigence between 1945 and 1949 and world sympathy with them during this period (**30**), and still underpins modern Israeli diplomacy (**88**).

1   Letter from Sir Henry McMahon to the Sherif Husein, 24 October 1915

. . . it is with great pleasure that I communicate to you on their behalf [the British government] the following statement, which I am confident that you will receive with satisfaction.

The two districts of Mersina and Alexandretta and portions of Syria lying to the west of the districts of Damascus, Homs, Hama and Aleppo cannot be said to be purely Arab, and should be excluded from the limits demanded.

With the above modification, and without prejudice to our existing treaties with Arab chiefs, we accept those limits.

As for those regions lying within those frontiers wherein Great Britain is free to act without detriment to the interests of her ally, France, I am empowered in the name of the Government of Great Britain to give the following assurances and make the following reply to your letter:

1 Subject to the above modifications, Great Britain is prepared to recognize and support the independence of the Arabs in all regions within the limits demanded by the Sherif of Mecca.

2 Great Britain will guarantee the Holy Places against all external aggression and will recognize their inviolability.

3 When the situation admits, Great Britain will give to the Arabs her advice and will assist them to establish what may appear to be the most suitable forms of government in those various territories.

4 On the other hand, it is understood that the Arabs have decided to seek the advice and guidance of Great Britain only, and that such European advisers and officials as may be required for the formation of a sound form of administration will be British.

5 With regard to the *vilayets* of Bagdad and Basra, the Arabs will recognize that the established position and interests of Great Britain necessitate special administrative arrangements in order to secure these territories from foreign aggression to promote the welfare of the local populations and to safeguard our mutual economic interests.

I am convinced that this declaration will assure you beyond all possible doubt of the sympathy of Great Britain towards the aspirations of her friends the Arabs and will result in a firm and lasting alliance, the immediate results of which will be the expulsion of the Turks from the Arab countries and the freeing of the Arab peoples from the Turkish yoke, which for so many years has pressed heavily upon them.

> *Correspondence between Sir Henry McMahon and the Sherif Hussein of Mecca, July 1915 – March 1916* (Cmd 5957, London, 1939)

2 British cabinet discussion on support for Zionism, 3 September 1917

2 The War Cabinet had under consideration correspondence which had passed between the Secretary of State for Foreign Affairs[1] and Lord Rothschild[2] on the question of the policy to be adopted towards the Zionist movement (G. T. – 1803). In addition to the draft declaration of policy included in the above correspondence, they had

---

1 Arthur James Balfour.
2 President of the English Zionist Federation.

before them an alternative draft prepared by Lord Milner (G.T. – 1803A). They also had before them a Memorandum by Mr Montagu[3] entitled 'The Anti-Semitism of the present Government'.

It was suggested that a question raising such important issues as to the future of Palestine ought, in the first instance, to be discussed with our Allies, and more particularly with the United States.

On the question of submitting Lord Milner's draft for the consideration of the United States Government, Mr Montagu urged that the use of the phrase 'the home of the Jewish people' would vitally prejudice the position of every Jew elsewhere and expand the argument contained in his Memorandum. Against this it was urged that the existence of a Jewish State or autonomous community in Palestine would strengthen rather than weaken the situation of Jews in countries where they were not yet in possession of equal rights, and that in countries like England, where they possessed such rights and were identified with the nation of which they were citizens, their position would be unaffected by the existence of a national Jewish community elsewhere. The view was expressed that, while a small influential section of English Jews were opposed to the idea, large numbers were sympathetic to it, but in the interests of Jews who wished to go from countries where they were less favourably situated, rather than from any idea of wishing to go to Palestine themselves.

With reference to a suggestion that the matter might be postponed, the Acting Secretary of State for Foreign Affairs pointed out that this was a question on which the Foreign Office had been very strongly pressed for a long time past. There was a very strong and enthusiastic organization, more particularly in the United States, who were zealous in this matter, and his belief was that it would be of most substantial assistance to the Allies to have the earnestness and enthusiasm of these people enlisted on our side. To do nothing was to risk a direct breach with them, and it was necessary to face this situation.

War Cabinet 227, CAB 23/4

3   Secretary of State for India.

3   British cabinet discussion on support for Zionism, 4 October
    1917

18   With reference to War Cabinet 227, Minute 2, the Secretary of
State for Foreign Affairs stated that the German Government were
making great efforts to capture the sympathy of the Zionist Movement. This Movement, though opposed by a number of wealthy Jews
in this country, had behind it the support of a majority of Jews, at all
events in Russia and America, and possibly in other countries. He saw
nothing inconsistent between the establishment of a Jewish national
focus in Palestine and the complete assimilation and absorption of
Jews into the nationality of other countries. Just as English emigrants
to the United States became, either in the first or subsequent generations, American nationals, so, in future, should a Jewish citizenship be
established in Palestine, would Jews become either Englishmen,
Americans, Germans, or Palestinians. What was at the back of the
Zionist Movement was the intense national consciousness held by
certain members of the Jewish race. They regarded themselves as one
of the great historic races of the world, whose original home was
Palestine, and these Jews had a passionate longing to regain once more
this ancient national home. Other Jews had become absorbed into the
nations among whom they and their forefathers had dwelt for many
generations. Mr Balfour then read a very sympathetic declaration by
the French Government which had been conveyed to the Zionists, and
he stated that he knew that President Wilson was extremely favourable
to the Movement.

Attention was drawn to the contradictory telegrams received from
Colonel House and Justice Brandeis (Papers G.T. − 2015 and
G.T. − 2158).

Mr Montagu urged strong objections to any declaration in which it
was stated that Palestine was the 'national home' of the Jewish people.
He regarded the Jews as a religious community and himself as a Jewish
Englishman. He based his argument on the prejudicial effect on the
status of Jewish Britons of a statement that His Majesty's Government
regarded Palestine as the national home of Jewish people. Whatever
safeguarding words might be used in the formula, the civil rights of
Jews as nationals in the country in which they were born might be
endangered. How could he negotiate with the peoples of India on
behalf of His Majesty's Government if the world had just been told that
His Majesty's Government regarded his national home as being in
Turkish territory? He specially urged that the only trial of strength

between Zionists and anti-Zionists in England had resulted in a very narrow majority for the Zionists, namely, 56 to 51, of the representatives of Anglo-Jewry on the Conjoint Committee. He also pointed out that most English-born Jews were opposed to Zionism, while it was supported by foreign-born Jews, such as Dr Caster and Dr Herz, the two Grand Rabbis, who had been born in Roumania and Austria respectively, and Dr Weizmann, President of the English Zionist Federation, who was born in Russia. He submitted that the Cabinet's first duty was to English Jews, and that Colonel House had declared that President Wilson is opposed to a declaration now.

Lord Curzon urged strong objections upon practical grounds. He stated, from his recollection of Palestine, that the country was, for the most part, barren and desolate; there being but sparse cultivation on the terraced slopes, the valleys and streams being few, and large centres of population scarce, a less propitious seat for the future Jewish race could not be imagined. How was it proposed to get rid of the existing majority of Mussulman inhabitants and to introduce the Jews in their place? How many would be willing to return and on what pursuits would they engage?

To secure for the Jews already in Palestine equal civil and religious rights seemed to him a better policy than to aim at repatriation on a large scale. He regarded the latter as sentimental idealism, which would never be realized, and that His Majesty's Government should have nothing to do with it.

It was pointed out that during recent years before the War, Jewish immigration into Palestine had been considerably on the increase, and that several flourishing Zionist colonies were already in existence.

Lord Milner submitted an alternative draft declaration, as follows:

'His Majesty's Government views with favour the establishment in Palestine of a National Home for the Jewish Race, and will use its best endeavours to facilitate the achievement of this object—it being clearly understood that nothing shall be done which may prejudice the civil and religious rights of the existing non-Jewish communities in Palestine, or the rights and political status in any other country by such Jews who are fully contented with their existing nationality and citizenship.'

The War Cabinet decided that—

Before coming to a decision they should hear the views of some of the representative Zionists, as well as of those who held the opposite opinion, and that meanwhile the declaration, as read by Lord Milner, should be submitted confidentially to—

(a) President Wilson.
(b) Leaders of the Zionist Movement.
(c) Representative persons in Anglo-Jewry opposed to Zionism.
The Secretary was instructed to take the necessary action. The War Cabinet further decided that the opinions received upon this draft declaration should be collated and submitted to them for decision.

War Cabinet 245, CAB 23/4

4 British cabinet discussion on support for Zionism, 31 October 1917

12 . . . The Secretary of State for Foreign Affairs stated that he gathered that everyone was now agreed that, from a purely diplomatic and political point of view, it was desirable that some declaration favourable to the aspiration of the Jewish nationalists should now be made. The vast majority of Jews in Russia and America, as, indeed, all over the world, now appeared to be favourable to Zionism. If we could make a declaration favourable to such an ideal, we should be able to carry on extremely useful propaganda both in Russia and America. He gathered that the main arguments still being put forward against Zionism were twofold:
(a) That Palestine was inadequate to form a home for either the Jewish or any other people.
(b) The difficulty felt with regard to the future position of Jews in Western countries.
With regard to the first, he understood that there were considerable differences of opinion among experts regarding the possibility of the settlement of any large population in Palestine, but he was informed that, if Palestine were scientifically developed, a very much larger population could be sustained than had existed during the period of Turkish misrule. As to the meaning of the words 'national home', to which the Zionists attach so much importance, he understood it to mean some form of British, American, or other protectorate, under which full facilities would be given to the Jews to work out their own salvation and to build up, by means of education, agriculture, and industry, a real centre of national culture and focus of national life. It did not necessarily involve the early establishment of an independent Jewish State, which was a matter for gradual development in accordance with the ordinary laws of political evolution.
With regard to the second point, he felt that, so far from Zionism hindering the process of assimilation in Western countries, the truer

parallel was to be found in the position of an Englishman who leaves his country to establish a permanent home in the United States. In the latter case there was no difficulty in the Englishman or his children becoming full nationals of the United States, whereas, in the present position of Jewry, the assimilation was often felt to be incomplete, and any danger of a double allegiance or non-national outlook would be eliminated.

Lord Curzon stated that he admitted the force of the diplomatic arguments in favour of expressing sympathy, and agreed that the bulk of the Jews held Zionist rather than anti-Zionist opinions, He added that he did not agree with the attitude taken up by Mr Montagu. On the other hand, he could not share the optimistic views held regarding the future of Palestine. These views were not merely the result of his own personal experiences of travel in that country, but of careful investigations from persons who had lived for many years in the country. He feared that by the suggested declaration we should be raising false expectations which could never be realized. He attached great importance to the necessity of retaining the Christian and Moslem Holy Places in Jerusalem and Bethlehem, and, if this were to be effectively done, he did not see how the Jewish people could have a political capital in Palestine. However, he recognized that some expression of sympathy with Jewish aspirations would be a valuable adjunct to our propaganda, though he thought that we should be guarded in the language used in giving expression to such sympathy.

The War Cabinet authorized –

The Secretary of State for Foreign Affairs to take a suitable opportunity of making the following declaration of sympathy with the Zionist aspirations: –

'His Majesty's Government views with favour the establishment in Palestine of a national home for the Jewish people, and will use its best endeavours to facilitate the achievement of this object, it being clearly understood that nothing shall be done which may prejudice the civil and religious rights of existing non-Jewish communities in Palestine, or the rights and political status enjoyed by Jews in any other country.'

War Cabinet 261, CAB 23/4

5   **Chaim Weizmann's analysis of Britain's motives for the Balfour declaration**

Like every human deed, the Balfour Declaration had two main

motives. There was no question but that it had an ideal nature. The statesmen of that time, Mr Balfour and Mr Lloyd George amongst them, primarily wanted to manifest a certain amount of restitution to the Jewish people for the contribution which the Jews have made in three thousands of years to the civilization of mankind which, you know, is common knowledge. Mr Lloyd George and Mr Balfour were deeply religious men and knew the Bible, knew the value of the Bible and the effect the Bible had on the character and the life of the British nation, and they could not help and were only too glad to connect this influence with the others or with the nation in the midst of whom the Bible was born.

I remember very well the first talk which I had with Mr Lloyd George—that was long before there was any talk of a Declaration or similar action—that he said, in a way half-jokingly and half-seriously—'You talk to me about Palestine. That is the only geography which I know, and I am acquainted with the geography of Palestine almost better than with the geography of the present front.' He was proud to be associated with this work, and there was no doubt an underlying ideal motive which moved the statesmen of that time—primarily the two foremost statesmen to issue the Declaration.

There was, as I said, another set of motives and they were utilitarian; not utilitarian in a gross or purely materialistic sense, as I am going to explain in a moment. We were—I mean the British people and those who were associated with the British, and I was associated with the British nation and proud to be so—all engaged in a war of life and death—which meant the existence or non-existence of the Commonwealth of Great Britain. A great deal depended upon America. In America there was a powerful Jewish community which was at that time, for some reason or other—I did not agree with this reason, but it was more or less current opinion in Great Britain at that time—either very neutral or inclined to be pro-German, some of them, the powerful Jews, or the Jews of German ancestry. It was thought that by this act of restitution—at any rate a form of declaration—this might swing the opinion of a powerful group of American Jewry.

There was another group—the Zionist group—which was never pro-German. It was always anxious to see British victory. But we wanted to have a united Jewish community of America standing behind the great war effort and behind President Wilson, who was carefully preparing his nation for entry into the war, for taking upon themselves a great ordeal, and it was thought that the Balfour

Declaration might help to swing the opinion of this community. I believe it had some effect, and I believe that in that respect it had fulfilled the purpose which was intended at that time.

There was also another community at that time which played a great part in the war — another Jewish community — and that was the Russian Jewish Community. It was, you remember, before Russia was divided and before Poland was re-established, and the Russian Jewish Community was the largest in the world. It was six million strong, and also the opinion of the Russian Jewish Community was of considerable value in that constellation of circumstances. There were two purposes; one was purely idealistic, and the other partly utilitarian.

UNSCOP *Report*, vol. III, verbatim hearing of the Twenty-First Meeting (Public), Jerusalem, 8 July 1947, hearing of Dr Weizmann

6   Lord Curzon to Colonel French, Cairo, 4 August 1919

Following is for your information and guidance and for that of all heads of administration and their local representatives:

His Majesty's Government's policy contemplates concession to Great Britain of Mandate for Palestine. Terms of Mandate will embody substance of declaration of 2 November 1917. Arabs will not be despoiled of their land nor required to leave the country. There is no question of majority being subjected to the rule of minority, nor does Zionist programme contemplate this.

All denominations will enjoy religious liberty and Holy Places of Christians and Mohammedans will remain in custody of adherents of those religions. American and French Governments are equally pledged to support in Palestine of Jewish national home. This should be emphasized to Arab leaders at every opportunity and it should be impressed upon them that the matter is a '*chose jugée*' and continued agitation would be useless and detrimental. Development of Palestine under new regime may be expected to involve large influx of money and all classes and races will benefit by its expenditure.

DBFP 1919 – 1939, First Series, vol. IV, (London, 1952), no. 236

7   Memorandum by Arthur Balfour, Paris, respecting Syria, Palestine, and Mesopotamia, 11 August 1919

The contradiction between the letter of the Covenant [of the

League of Nations] and the policy of the Allies is even more flagrant in the case of the 'independent nation' of Syria. For in Palestine we do not propose even to go through the form of consulting the wishes of the present inhabitants of the country, though the American Commission has been going through the form of asking what they are. The four Great Powers are committed to Zionism. And Zionism, be it right or wrong, good or bad, is rooted in age-long traditions, in present needs, in future hopes, of far profounder import than the desires and prejudices of the 700,000 Arabs who now inhabit that ancient land.

DBFP 1919 – 1939, First Series, vol. IV, no. 242

8   The Churchill White Paper, June 1922

The tension which has prevailed from time to time in Palestine is mainly due to apprehensions, which are entertained both by sections of the Arab and by sections of the Jewish population. These apprehensions, so far as the Arabs are concerned, are partly based upon exaggerated interpretations of the meaning of the Declaration favouring the establishment of a Jewish National Home in Palestine, made on behalf of His Majesty's Government on 2 November, 1917. Unauthorized statements have been made to the effect that the purpose in view is to create a wholly Jewish Palestine. Phrases have been used such as that Palestine is to become 'as Jewish as England is English'. His Majesty's Government regard any such expectation as impracticable and have no such aim in view. Nor have they at any time contemplated, as appears to be feared by the Arab Delegation, the disappearance or the subordination of the Arabic population, language, or culture in Palestine. They would draw attention to the fact that the terms of the Declaration referred to do not contemplate that Palestine as a whole should be converted into a Jewish National Home, but that such a Home should be founded *in Palestine*. When it is asked what is meant by the development of the Jewish National Home in Palestine, it may be answered that it is not the imposition of a Jewish nationality upon the inhabitants of Palestine as a whole, but the further development of the existing Jewish community, with the assistance of Jews in other parts of the world, in order that it may become a centre in which the Jewish people as a whole may take, on grounds of religion and race, an interest and a pride. But in order that this community should have the best prospect of free development and provide a full opportunity for the Jewish people to display its capacities, it is essential that it should know that it is in Palestine as of right and not on sufferance. That is the reason why it is necessary that the existence of a Jewish National Home in Palestine should be internationally guaranteed, and that it should be formally recognized to rest upon ancient historic connection.

This, then, is the interpretation which His Majesty's Government place upon the Declaration of 1917, and, so understood, the Secretary of State is of opinion that it does not contain or imply anything which need cause either alarm to the Arab population or disappointment to the Jews.

Statement of British Policy in Palestine,
3 June 1922 (Cmd. 1700, 1922)

9 The Peel Commission's justification for proposing partition for Palestine, 1937

An irrepressible conflict has arisen between two national communities within the narrow bounds of one small country. About 1,000,000 Arabs are in strife, open or latent, with some 400,000 Jews. There is no common ground between them. The Arab community is predominantly Asiatic in character, the Jewish community predominantly European. They differ in religion and in language. Their cultural and social life, their ways of thought and conduct, are as incompatible as their national aspirations. These last are the greatest bar to peace. Arabs and Jews might possibly learn to live and work together in Palestine if they would make a genuine effort to reconcile and combine their national ideals and so build up in time a joint or dual nationality. But this they cannot do. The War and its sequel have inspired all Arabs with the hope of reviving in a free and united Arab world the traditions of the Arab golden age. The Jews similarly are inspired by their historic past. They mean to show what the Jewish nation can achieve when restored to the land of its birth. National assimilation between Arabs and Jews is thus ruled out. In the Arab picture the Jews could only occupy the place they occupied in Arab Egypt or Arab Spain. The Arabs would be as much outside the Jewish picture as the Canaanites in the old land of Israel. The National Home, as we have said before, cannot be half-national. In these circumstances to maintain that Palestinian citizenship has any moral meaning is a mischievous pretence. Neither Arab nor Jew has any sense of service to a single State.

Palestine Royal Commission Report,
(Cmd. 5479, 1937)

10   The 1939 White Paper on Palestine

In the light of these considerations His Majesty's Government make the following declaration of their intentions regarding the future government of Palestine:

(1) The objective of His Majesty's Government is the establishment within ten years of an independent Palestine State in such treaty relations with the United Kingdom as will provide satisfactorily for the commercial and strategic requirements of both countries in the future. The proposal for the establishment of the independent State would involve consultation with the Council of the League of Nations with a view to the termination of the Mandate.

(2) The independent State should be one in which Arabs and Jews share in government in such a way as to ensure that the essential interests of each community are safeguarded.

.   .   .

14   It has been urged that all further Jewish immigration into Palestine should be stopped forthwith. His Majesty's Government cannot accept such a proposal. It would damage the whole of the financial and economic system of Palestine and thus affect adversely the interests of Arabs and Jews alike. Moreover, in the view of His Majesty's Government, abruptly to stop further immigration would be unjust to the Jewish National Home. But, above all, His Majesty's Government are conscious of the present unhappy plight of large numbers of Jews who seek a refuge from certain European countries, and they believe that Palestine can and should make a further contribution to the solution of this pressing world problem. In all these circumstances, they believe that they will be acting consistently with their Mandatory obligations to both Arabs and Jews, and in the manner best calculated to serve the interests of the whole people of Palestine, by adopting the following proposals regarding immigration:

(1) Jewish immigration during the next five years will be at a rate which, if economic absorptive capacity permits, will bring the Jewish

population up to approximately one-third of the total population of the country. Taking into account the expected natural increase of the Arab and Jewish populations, and the number of illegal Jewish immigrants now in the country, this would allow of the admission, as from the beginning of April this year, of some 75,000 immigrants over the next five years. These immigrants would, subject to the criterion of economic absorptive capacity, be admitted as follows:

(a) For each of the next five years a quota of 10,000 Jewish immigrants will be allowed on the understanding that a shortage in any one year may be added to the quotas for subsequent years, within the five-year period, if economic absorptive capacity permits.

(b) In addition, as a contribution towards the solution of the Jewish refugee problem, 25,000 refugees will be admitted as soon as the High Commissioner is satisfied that adequate provision for their maintenance is ensured, special consideration being given to refugee children and dependants.

(2) The existing machinery for ascertaining economic absorptive capacity will be retained, and the High Commissioner will have the ultimate responsibility for deciding the limits of economic capacity. Before each periodic decision is taken, Jewish and Arab representatives will be consulted.

(3) After the period of five years no further Jewish immigration will be permitted unless the Arabs of Palestine are prepared to acquiesce in it.

(4) His Majesty's Government are determined to check illegal immigration, and further preventive measures are being adopted. The numbers of any Jewish illegal immigrants who, despite these measures, may succeed in coming into the country and cannot be deported will be deducted from the yearly quotas.

15 His Majesty's Government are satisfied that, when the immigration over five years which is now contemplated has taken place, they will not be justified in facilitating, nor will they be under any obligation to facilitate, the further development of the Jewish National Home by immigration regardless of the wishes of the Arab population.

Palestine: Statement of Policy, (Cmd. 6019, 1939)

11 SS Sturmbannführer Dr Wilhelm Hoettl on the numbers killed in Hitler's 'final solution'

At the end of August 1944 I was talking to SS-Obersturmbannführer Adolf Eichmann, whom I had known since 1938. The conversation took place in my home in Budapest.

.   .   .

He expressed his conviction that Germany had now lost the war and that he, personally, had no further chance. He knew that he would be considered one of the main war criminals by the United Nations since he had millions of Jewish lives on his conscience. I asked him how many that was, to which he answered that although the number was a great Reich secret, he would tell me since I, as a historian, would be interested and that he would probably not return anyhow from his command in Rumania. He had, shortly before that, made a report to Himmler, as the latter wanted to know the exact number of Jews who had been killed. On the basis of his information he had obtained the following result:

Approximately four million Jews had been killed in the various extermination camps while an additional two million met death in other ways, the major part of which were shot by operational squads of the Security Police during the campaign against Russia.

Nazi Conspiracy and Aggression, vol. V,
document 2738 – PS

12 Rudolf Hoess on the methods of the 'final solution'

The 'final solution' of the Jewish question meant the complete extermination of all Jews in Europe. I was ordered to establish extermination facilities at Auschwitz in June 1941. At that time there were already in the general government[1] three other extermination camps: Belzek, Treblinka and Wolzek. These camps were under the Einsatzkommando of the Security Police and SD. I visited Treblinka to find out how they carried out their extermination. The Camp Commandant at Treblinka told me he had liquidated 80,000 in the course of one-half year. He was principally concerned with liquidating all the Jews from the Warsaw ghetto. He used monoxide gas and I did not think that his methods were very efficient. So when I set up the extermination building at Auschwitz, I used Cyclon B, which was a crystallized prussic acid which we dropped into the death chamber from a small opening. It took from 3 to 15 minutes to kill the people in

1 Nazi occupied Poland.

the death chamber depending upon climatic conditions. We knew when the people were dead because their screaming stopped. We usually waited about one-half hour before we opened the doors and removed the bodies. After the bodies were removed our special commandos took off the rings and extracted the gold from the teeth of the corpses.

Nazi Conspiracy and Aggression, vol. VI, document 3868-PS

II

The Overthrow of British Power in Palestine

At the end of the second world war, Britain sought to maintain some kind of imperial presence in the Middle East, but lacked the military and economic strength to do so. The competing Zionist groups in Palestine were united in their determination to harry Britain into relinquishing her mandate with as little delay as possible. On 13 November 1945, under pressure from Washington and faced with the outbreak of violence the previous month by the Haganah, the Irgun and the Sternists, the British government announced the appointment of the Anglo-American Committee of Inquiry, whose conclusions are summarized in document 13. Document 14 indicates some of the reasons why Clement Attlee's government ultimately came to consider these recommendations unacceptable, setting out some of the sobering realities which underlay the weakness of Britain's post-war position in Palestine. In document 15 the American Joint Chiefs of Staff argue against acceding to Britain's request for the military assistance she considered a prerequisite for the implementation of the Anglo-American Committee's scheme. It is interesting that by this time American service chiefs were viewing the Middle East in the contexts of its importance as an oil supplier and its geographical relation to the incipient Cold War with the Soviet Union. The Committee's proposals in the end came to nothing but this period of uncertainty did not solve Britain's dilemma as the increasingly troubled mandatory power.

During the period when the Anglo-American Committee's report was being discussed between London and Washington, the authorities in Palestine tried to curb the growing violence by occupying the offices of the Jewish Agency, ordering the arrest of some of its leaders, and initiating searches for Haganah arms. On 22 July 1946, the Irgun, with Haganah concurrence, blew up the wing of the King David Hotel in Jerusalem which housed the British military and civil headquarters (16). The dramatic nature of this challenge emphasized the necessity to work quickly for a political solution, particularly one which would attract American support. But the British government did not find President Truman's interventions helpful, and documents 17 and 18 trace their final attempt to reach a political agreement between the two main parties to the Palestinian dispute. Earlier discussions in September 1946 between Britain and the Arab states had been adjourned. When the conference resumed in London on 27 January 1947, the Arab Higher Committee, representing the Palestinians, took part and members of the Jewish Agency also held separate discussions with the government. On 14 February 1947, the Foreign Secretary, Ernest Bevin, on whom the chief burden and opprobrium of the final phase of Britain's Palestinian policy had fallen, reported the failure of either side to favour the plan the cabinet had sanctioned the previous week (17) and recommended that his colleagues implement their threat to refer the problem to the United Nations (18). This request was conveyed to the organization's Secretary-General on 2 April; the fate of Palestine was to be decided in a wider, and largely untried, forum.

13 Dean Acheson, Acting Secretary of State, to certain American diplomatic and consular officers summarizing the conclusions of the Anglo-American Committee of Inquiry, 25 April 1946

Report Anglo-Am Committee Inquiry re Palestine will be published 1 May according to present plans. Summary of main conclusions for your strictly confidential info follows:

1   No hope in countries other than Palestine of substantial assistance in finding homes Jews wishing or forced leave Europe. But this is world responsibility and Palestine alone cannot meet Jewish emigration needs. AmBrit Govts in association other countries should endeavor find new homes all displaced and nonrepatriable persons both Jews, non-Jews. Since most will continue live Europe, AmBrit Govts should endeavor secure basic human rights freedoms as set forth UN Charter.

2   100,000 certificates for Jewish victims Nazi Fascist persecution should be authorized immediately for admission Palestine. Certificates awarded as far possible 1946 and actual immigration accelerated as rapidly conditions permit.

3   Exclusive claims of Jews and Arabs to Palestine shall be disposed of once for all on three principles: Jew shall not dominate Arab in

Palestine and vice versa; Palestine shall be neither Jewish nor Arab state; form of govt ultimately established shall fully protect interests of Christian, Jewish, Moslem faiths under international guarantees. Ultimately Palestine to become state guarding interests of Moslems, Jews and Christians alike according fullest measure selfgovt consistent three principles above. Palestine as Holy Land completely different from others hence narrow nationalism inappropriate. In view ancient [and] recent history Pal neither purely Arab nor Jewish land. Jewish National Home has right to continued existence protection development. Minority guarantees would not afford adequate protection for subordinated group. Struggle for numerical majority must be made hopeless by constitution.

4   Hostile feeling between Jews Arabs and determination of both achieve domination makes almost certain attempt establish Palestinian state or states now or some time to come would result in civil strife possible threatening world peace. Palestine Govt should continue under mandate then UN trusteeship until hostility disappears.

5   Mandatory or trustee should declare Arab economic, educational, political advancement in Palestine equal importance with Jewish and prepare measures bridge present gap by raising Arab standards. Perhaps advisable encourage formation Arab community on lines Jewish community.

6   Pending trusteeship agreement Mandatory should facilitate Jewish immigration while ensuring rights and position of other sections of population not prejudiced. In future Pal Govt should have right decide number immigrants admitted in any period having regard to well-being Pal people. View disapproved that any Jew anywhere can enter Pal as of right. Any immigrant Jew entering Pal contrary its law is illegal immigrant.

7   Land transfers regulations should be amended on basis freedom sale, lease, use of land irrespective race, community, creed. Stipulations that only members one race, community, creed may be employed in connection conveyances, leases, agreements should be made nugatory and prohibited. Govt should closely supervise holy places and localities to protect desecration offensive uses.

8   Not competent assess value plans presented for agricultrual industrial development. Such projects if successful of great benefit but require peace and cooperation adjacent Arab states. Full consultation, cooperation required from start with Jewish Agency and Arab states affected.

9   Reformation of education system both Jews Arabs and introduc-
tion compulsory education.
10   Should be made clear beyond doubt to both Jews Arabs that
attempts by violence, threats, organization or use illegal armies to
prevent execution of report will be resolutely suppressed. Jewish
Agency should resume cooperation with Mandatory suppress
terrorism, illegal immigration, maintain law order.

                                    FRUS 1946, vol. VII, pp. 585 – 6, 867N.
                                    01/4 – 2546

14   Secretary of State James F. Byrnes to President Harry S. Truman on British policy in Palestine after the Anglo-American Committee of Inquiry, 9 May 1946

For the President from the Secretary. Bevin has given me a copy of a
memorandum prepared by his Govt for his use in discussing the Anglo-
American Committee's report on Palestine and the Jewish question of
which the following is a summary:
1   A brief examination shows that the commitments involved in
giving effect to the report would involve the expenditure of large sums
of money and the employment of military forces to an extent beyond
the capacity of His Majesty's Govt to meet alone. Before any decision is
taken as to whether the report should be put into force or not the
British Govt must know what assistance they can count on obtaining
from the US Govt.
2   The military burden is the more important one. Before any
decision could be taken to admit 100,000 additional immigrants as
recommended in the report, the illegal Jewish armies must be
suppressed and there must be a general disarmament throughout
Palestine. Otherwise these armies would be swollen by recruits drawn
from the new immigrants. The implementation of the report would
cause serious repercussions throughout the Arab world involving
additional military commitments which the British Govt could not
undertake alone in present circumstances.
3   The British now have an equivalent of two and one-half divisions
in Palestine. The British Govt considers that adoption of the
Committee's report would make necessary reinforcements of the order
of two infantry divisions and one armoured brigade. There is no
possibility of providing these reinforcements from British sources if
they are to meet their inescapable commitments in other parts of the

world. It would be necessary for American forces of the required strength to be immediately available before the policy recommended could be endorsed by the British Govt, and it would be essential to obtain a guarantee that American assistance would be sustained at full strength so long as the commitment in Palestine lasted. A token contingent would not be sufficient.

4   A conservative estimate is that the recommendations of the report would involve an expenditure of from 60,000,000 to 70,000,000 pounds in Palestine during the next couple of years if the new immigrants are to be housed and fitted into the economy of the country. Over a period of 10 years the expenditure involved would be from 115,000,000 to 125,000,000 pounds. The foregoing figures exclude the cost of development schemes such as the Jordan Valley project which is estimated to cost 76,000,000 pounds.

5   Zionists have suggested that expenditures of this nature be met from reparations allocation for the victims of Nazism but the total available from this source for both Jews and non-Jews is only about 7,500,000 pounds. Even allowing for a maximum effort by world Jewry, there will obviously be a much larger residue than the British Govt will be able to bear alone and it would be glad to know to what extent it can count on American financial assistance should it be decided to put these measures into operation.

6   The British are convinced that they would not be in a position to put the report into operation without substantial financial and military contributions from the US Govt.

7   Both the British and US Govts are committed to consultation with the Arabs and Jews before a new policy is adopted which fact would preclude the British Govt from giving immediate effect to the report.

8   Consideration should be given to the form of such consultation and whether the US would be associated with the British Govt in conducting them.

9   If the US Govt is unable to agree to assist in implementing the report the British Govt will have to consider what its future policy in Palestine is to be. Meanwhile some other state may refer the matter to the Security Council at any moment as a situation likely to endanger the maintenance of international peace and security.

10   The British Govt considers that the Committee on Refugees and Displaced Persons of the Economic and Social Council should deal with the question of the disposal of the Jews for whom immigration to Palestine has been suggested.

FRUS 1946, vol VII, pp. 601 – 3,
740.00119 Council/5 – 946: Telegram

15 Memorandum from the American Joint Chiefs of Staff to the
    State-War-Navy Coordinating Committee, 21 June 1946

With regard to the request of 7 June by the Acting State member,
State-War-Navy Coordinating Committee (Appendix), following are
comments by the Joint Chiefs of Staff on certain topics proposed by the
British for joint consideration in connection with the recommendations of the report of the Anglo-American Committee of Inquiry on
Palestine. It will be noted that no definitive recommendations are
offered on many of the difficult political aspects of this problem, on
which the Joint Chiefs of Staff do not feel they should advise.

We urge that no US armed forces be involved in carrying out the
Committee's recommendations. We recommend that in implementing the report, the guiding principle be that no action should be taken
which will cause repercussions in Palestine which are beyond the
capabilities of British troops to control.

Should the question of using any US forces arise, we would point out
that, under present War and Navy Department commitments to the
Congress, only very limited forces could be spared from tasks in which
we are already engaged. Such contingents might in theory be of a size
to contribute to pacifying the situation *in Palestine*, but we believe
that the political shock attending the reappearance of US armed
forces in the Middle East would unnecessarily risk such serious disturbances throughout the area as to dwarf any local Palestine difficulties. Such a condition would, among other effects, invalidate entirely
any current estimates of required strengths of the Army and Navy.
Further, the Middle East could well fall into anarchy and become a
breeding ground for world war.

It is believed that implementation of the report by force would
prejudice British and US interests in much of the Middle East and that
British and US influence would consequently be curtailed except as it
might be maintained by military force. The USSR might replace the
United States and Britain in influence and power throughout the
Middle East.

As to the importance of a stable Middle East, friendly to the
Western Powers, it is obvious that this area is the buffer between
Russia and the British Mediterranean life-line. If the peoples of the
Middle East turn to Russia, this would have the same impact in many
respects as would military conquest of this area by the Soviets. Under
these conditions, even if Turkey maintains her internal and political
integrity, it is highly questionable that she should continue her stand

on the Dardanelles and maintain her position as other than a satellite Russian state. Also, for very serious consideration from a military point of view is control of the oil of the Middle East. This is probably the one large undeveloped reserve in a world which may come to the limits of its oil resources within this generation without having developed any substitute. A great part of our military strength, as well as our standard of living, is based on oil.

As to US participation in a Palestine trusteeship, we consider that military advice must rest on our supposition that such participation would lead to military involvement, on which subject our views are stated above.

In summary, the Joint Chiefs of Staff recommend that in implementing the report of the Anglo-American Committee, no action be taken which would:

(a) Commit US armed forces, or

(b) Orient the people of the Middle East away from the Western Powers, as the US has a vital security interest in that area.

FRUS 1946, vol. VII, pp. 631 – 3, 867N.
01/7 – 246

16 British cabinet discussion following the attack on the King David Hotel, 23 July 1946

The Secretary of State for the Colonies[1] gave the Cabinet the latest information about the explosion which had occurred on the previous day in the Headquarters of the Government Secretariat and Army Command in the King David Hotel, Jerusalem.

It appeared that a lorry had been driven up to the tradesmen's entrance of the hotel; and that the occupants, after holding up the staff at the pistol point, had entered the kitchen premises carrying a number of milk cans. They had shot and seriously wounded a British soldier who had challenged them; and, after placing bombs in the basement of the building, had made good their escape. The subsequent explosion had destroyed a substantial part of the building. The casualties so far reported were 41 killed, 52 missing and 53 injured.

The Officer Administering the Government in the absence of the High Commissioner had reported that a large proportion of his staff

1 George Hall.

were dead, missing or wounded, and that this created a situation which could be handled only if drastic action were taken by His Majesty's Government. He had consulted his Executive Council and the General Officer Commanding the troops in Palestine, and they were agreed that only two alternative courses were open. The first was to institute widespread searches for arms with a view to breaking up the Jewish resistance movement. This, in their view, would create conditions tantamount to a state of war in Palestine. The second alternative was for His Majesty's Government to announce a final solution of the political problem. This was the alternative which they preferred. In view of this latest outrage, further negotiations with the Jews seemed to be impossible; and the best course would be for His Majesty's Government to impose their own solution of the political problem.

The Prime Minister[2] said that, although there was evidence that the Haganah had been implicated in some of the earlier acts of violence, there was no reason to believe that any but the most extreme advocates of violence were involved in this latest outrage. Our earlier action against Jewish illegal organizations had had the effect of strengthening the influence of the more moderate Jewish leaders in Palestine; and it would be a mistake to rush into a widespread search for arms, which would be taken as a measure directed against all the Jews in Palestine, before we had any evidence to show who had been responsible for this latest outrage. Such action might have the effect of alienating all sections of Jewish opinion in Palestine. On the other hand, he thought it would equally be a mistake for His Majesty's Government to take a sudden decision on the political problem, before the consultations with the United States Government had been completed. In his view the right course was to press on with the Anglo-American conversations and to seek an early agreement with the United States Government on a long-term policy. If such an agreement could be reached, we should announce our joint policy and try to rally the support of world opinion in favour of its adoption.

The Foreign Secretary[3] said that he also attached importance to securing an early declaration by the United States Government condemning this recent outrage. He had already suggested that such a declaration should be made and he hoped that it might be made very shortly.

In discussion there was general agreement with the views expressed

2   Clement Attlee.
3   Ernest Bevin.

by the Prime Minister. In particular, the Cabinet agreed that it would be a mistake to break off the discussions with the United States Government. These discussions were going very well and it seemed probable that agreed conclusions on the general principles of a settlement could be formulated by the following day. The United States Delegation hoped to be able to obtain the approval of their Government to these agreed conclusions by the end of the week; if not, it should be possible for the Foreign Secretary very shortly afterwards to discuss them with the United States Secretary of State in Paris and to obtain agreement on them there. It had previously been the intention that the results of the discussions with the United States Delegation should not be published before the proposed conference with Arab and Jewish representatives. In the altered circumstances, however — and particularly now that statements had appeared in the Press which foreshadowed part of the conclusions — the Cabinet felt that it would be advisable that they should be published as soon as possible. They must first be conveyed to the Arab Governments and to the representatives of the Jews, but it might be possible for this to be done in time for an announcement to be made before or during the debate which was to take place before the Summer Recess.

CAB 128/6 72(46)

17 British cabinet discussion on the final attempt to secure an agreed solution for Palestine, 7 February 1947

The Cabinet considered a joint memorandum by the Foreign Secretary and the Secretary of State for the Colonies (C.P. (47)49) reporting the progress of the discussions with Arab and Jewish representatives about the future of Palestine, and seeking authority to put before them as a basis for further negotiation the fresh proposals outlined in the Appendix to the memorandum.

The Foreign Secretary said that it was clear from the discussions that the Arabs were implacably opposed to Partition. Apart from their opposition, there would be grave practical difficulties in giving effect to Partition; and it was also doubtful whether any scheme of Partition which would be acceptable to the Jews would be regarded by His Majesty's Government as defensible. The Arabs also demanded that there should be no further Jewish immigration into Palestine; but on this point there should be some room for compromise if means could be found of allaying the Arab fears that, by immigration, the Jews would achieve a numerical majority in Palestine.

The Jews claimed that the Balfour Declaration and the Mandate implied a promise that a Jewish State would be established in the whole of Palestine. They were willing to consider as as compromise the creation of 'a viable Jewish State in an adequate area of Palestine'. The essential point of principle for the Jews was the creation of a sovereign Jewish State.

In these circumstances the Colonial Secretary and he had tried to find a solution which, even though it were not accepted by either community, was one which His Majesty's Government could conscientiously support and in which the two communities might finally acquiesce. They now sought authority to put before the Arabs and the Jews the plan outlined in the Appendix to C.P. (47)49. This had as its primary object the establishment of self-government in Palestine leading to independence after a transition period of five years under Trusteeship. It provided for a substantial measure of local autonomy in Arab and Jewish areas, and enabled Arabs and Jews to collaborate together at the centre. It contained special safeguards for the 'human rights' of the two communities. It provided for the admission of 100,000 Jewish immigrants over the next two years and for continued immigration thereafter by agreement between the two communities or, failing that, by arbitration under the United Nations. The plan incorporated features of many earlier schemes. It was consistent with the Mandate and, if it commanded a reasonable measure of acquiescence from either of the two communities, it could be set on foot at once and regularized subsequently by a Trusteeship Agreement.

If it were found that a plan on these lines was likely to command such a measure of acquiescence, the Cabinet would be asked to decide whether His Majesty's Government should go ahead with it. If on the other hand there was no prospect of acquiescence, it would then be necessary to submit the whole problem to the United Nations, explaining the various efforts which had been made to find a solution but making no recommendations.

.   .   .

The Secretary of State for the Colonies[1] said that he had previously thought that Partition afforded the only way out of the present deadlock in Palestine; and he had been confirmed in that opinion by the views expressed to him by the High Commissioner and by his

1   Arthur Creech Jones.

advisers in the Colonial Office. He confessed, however, that, the longer he had examined the detailed implications of Partition, the more he was impressed by its practical difficulties. It would be very difficult to establish a viable Jewish State without prejudicing the vital interests of the Palestine Arabs; and wherever the frontiers were drawn, large numbers of Arabs must inevitably, be left under Jewish rule. He was also impressed by the difficulties of securing the assent of the United Nations to a scheme of Partition. But perhaps the greatest difficulty of all was that the enforcement of Partition was, he was now convinced, bound to involve conditions of rebellion and disorder in Palestine which might last for a considerable time and would involve a substantial military commitment for us.

He was therefore in full agreement with the proposals in C.P. (47)49, which had been explained to the Cabinet by the Foreign Secretary. He believed that these proposals would go some way to meet the Jewish point of view on immigration and on land transfer. There were signs of some division of opinion among the leaders of the Jewish Agency, and some elements in the Jewish community here and in the United States considered that the Agency's demands were too extreme. He therefore hoped that the Jews might regard this plan as one which they were prepared to discuss.

.   .   .

It was pointed out that the proposals now put forward were based on the hope that Jews and Arabs would collaborate in a unitary State. This had been the foundation of our policy for many years but no signs had been forthcoming of any readiness to collaborate. Would this fresh attempt to secure collaboration meet with any more success?

The general view of Ministers was that, nevertheless, these was every advantage in putting forward these proposals to both parties as a basis for negotiation. The results of the further discussions would be reported to the Cabinet. It was also agreed that the negotiations must be brought to a point within the next week or so. If there was no measure of acquiescence in the proposals, then it seemed that reference to the United Nations would be necessary.

The Cabinet —

1   Authorized the Foreign Secretary and the Secretary of State for the Colonies to put before the representatives of the Arabs and the Jews the proposals outlined in the Appendix to C.P. (47)49 on the understanding that if an agreement were reached on this basis, His Majesty's Government would proceed to give effect to it.

2   Took note that, if in these further discussions no agreement were

reached, the Foreign Secretary would report to the Cabinet whether in their judgement these proposals were likely to meet with any substantial measure of acquiescence from either of the two communities in Palestine, and would then invite the Cabinet to decide whether His Majesty's Government would be justified in bringing the scheme into operation on their own authority pending the negotiation of a Trusteeship Agreement.

CAB 128/9 18(47)

18 British cabinet discussion on the breakdown of negotiations and their decision to refer the Palestine problem to the United Nations, 14 February 1947

The Cabinet considered a memorandum by the Foreign Secretary and the Secretary of State for the Colonies (C.P. (47)59) reporting the results of the further discussions with representatives of the Arabs and the Jews on the future of Palestine.

Both the Arabs and the Jews had declined to accept as a basis for further negotiations the proposals approved by the Cabinet on 7 February. The Jews had rejected them as likely to lead to an independent unitary State in which Jews would be a permanent minority. The Arabs had rejected them as leading inevitably to Partition and also because they provided for further Jewish immigration.

In these circumstances, it was recommended that His Majesty's Government should give immediate notice of their intention to refer the problem of Palestine to the judgement of the General Assembly of the United Nations. In placing the question before the Assembly His Majesty's Government should give an historical account of the discharge of their trust in Palestine, and should explain the various solutions which had been proposed; and, without themselves making any recommendations, should invite the Assembly to find a solution of the problem. The next Session of the Assembly would not be held until September, but it would probably be impracticable to arrange for a special Session to be held before then. Meanwhile, we must continue to administer the existing Mandate.

The Foreign Secretary recalled the various stages of the negotiations over the past eighteen months, and explained how the problem had become progressively more intractable. American Jewry now had great influence in the counsels of the Jewish Agency. He had made every effort to secure the assistance of the United States Government, but in the event their interventions had only increased our difficulties. When the first session of the London Conference had ended last autumn, he had not been without hope of a solution, but since then opinion on each side had hardened and the negotiations which had just taken place left no room for hope of a settlement acceptable to His Majesty's Government in which either side would acquiesce.

In the final stage of the negotiations the Jewish representatives had been prepared to consider a scheme of Partition, but when asked to define what they meant by their claim to a 'viable State in an adequate area of Palestine' they had made it clear that they claimed a far larger share than any which His Majesty's Government would be justified in proposing for the Jews under a Partition scheme. A map indicating the extent of the Jewish claim was shown to the Cabinet.

Further discussion showed that it was the general view of the Cabinet that the right course was now to submit the whole problem to the United Nations, on the basis proposed in C.P. (47)59. This submission would not involve an immediate surrender of the Mandate; but His Majesty's Government would not be under an obligation themselves to enforce whatever solution the United Nations might approve. If the settlement suggested by the United Nations were not acceptable to us, we should be at liberty then to surrender the Mandate and leave the United Nations to make other arrangements for the future administration of Palestine.

CAB 128/9 22(47)

III

The United Nations and the Partition of Palestine

The United Nations Special Committee on Palestine (UNSCOP), consisting of representatives of Australia, Canada, Czechoslovakia, Guatemala, India, Iran, the Netherlands, Peru, Sweden, Uruguay and Yugoslavia, was instituted by the United Nations General Assembly on 15 May 1947. Having investigated 'all questions and issues relevant to the problem of Palestine', it was to report back to the General Assembly with its recommendations by 1 September. During the Committee's visit to Palestine, two incidents impressed its members with the bankruptcy of the British administration. In July, the Irgun hanged two British servicemen in retaliation for the execution of its members, and there was also played out the spectacular drama of the Haganah refugee ship, *Exodus 1947* (formerly *President Warfield*) (**19, 20**). Document **21** gives the basis of UNSCOP's proposed solution, partition with economic union, which was supported by Canada, Czechoslovakia, Guatemala, the Netherlands, Peru, Sweden and Uruguay, but the scheme was unacceptable to the British government which was resolved to do nothing to assist with its implementation (**22**).

Prolonged discussion of UNSCOP's findings took place in the *Ad Hoc* Committee on the Palestinian Question, which included all General Assembly members. It was immediately apparent that a decision would largely depend upon the attitudes taken up by the Soviet Union and the United States, whose general policy is outlined in document **23**. Reversing its ill-advised decision to boycott UNSCOP, the Arab Higher Committee decided to state its position before the *Ad Hoc* Committee (**24**). The Jewish Agency's response to its arguments and to the UNSCOP recommendations are given in document **25**. After hearing the initial submissions, the committee divided into two sub-committees. Sub-Committee 2, consisting of Afghanistan, Colombia, Egypt, Iraq, Lebanon, Pakistan, Saudi Arabia, Syria and Yemen, reported in favour of a 'unitary, democratic and independent

State, with adequate safeguards for minorities'. Sub-Committee 1, led by the United States and the Soviet Union, but also comprising Canada, Czechoslovakia, Guatemala, Poland, South Africa, Uruguay and Venezuela, sought to find a means of implementing UNSCOP's partition recommendations (26). Its initial proposals had to be revised in the light of Britain's continuing attitude of non-cooperation (27, 28). As amended, Sub-Committee 1's recommendations were adopted by the *Ad Hoc* Committee on 25 November 1947 by twenty-five votes to thirteen, with seventeen abstentions. Such a vote made the necessary two-thirds majority in the imminent formal General Assembly appear problematic. During the Assembly meetings, from 26 to 29 November, Arab and Islamic countries continued to assert their total rejection of the idea of partition (29), while powerful advocacy and pressure from the Soviet Union (30) and the United States (31, 32) helped ensure its acceptance by a vote of thirty-three to thirteen, with ten abstentions.

The United Nations resolution of 29 November 1947 looked forward to a progressive transfer of power from the British mandatory authorities to a Palestine Commission, which would establish the frontiers of the Arab and Jewish states and of the city of Jerusalem. Because of Arab rejection of partition and, more especially, long-standing British refusal to cooperate, the Commission could do nothing (33). In the absence of any mechanism to implement the resolution, the Palestinian situation deteriorated rapidly with Arab and Jewish forces fighting to assert control over strategic areas. Atrocities were perpetrated by each side, the most notorious being the massacre carried out by Irgun and Stern members at the Arab village of Deir Yassin (34), in retaliation for which seventy-seven members of a Jewish medical convoy were killed on 12 April 1948.

19 British cabinet discussion of the difficulties facing the Palestine administration during the period of UNSCOP's inquiry, 31 July 1947

The Foreign Secretary recalled that, in spite of our efforts to prevent it, the *President Warfield* had succeeded in sailing for Palestine from a French port with some 4,500 illegal immigrants on board. These Jews had secured forged Colombian travel documents; and the ship itself had sailed without proper clearance. He had taken the matter up immediately with M. Bidault, who had agreed that, if we were successful in intercepting the ship, her passengers might be returned to France. The *President Warfield* had been intercepted off the Palestine coast by a naval patrol and her passengers transferred to three other ships, which were now in harbour at Port de Bouc. The illegal immigrants had, however, refused to disembark voluntarily and it was clear that, without the cooperation of the French authorities, it would be impossible to compel them to do so. His Majesty's Ambassador at Paris had reported that the French Government were not prepared to afford such cooperation, and that further representations to them would be unlikely to produce any successful results. In these circumstances he had discussed with the other Ministers concerned what alternative arrangements might be made for the disposal of the illegal immigrants. It had been agreed that there could be no question of sending them to Palestine or Cyprus, and the Secretary of State for the Colonies was considering whether accommodation could be found for them in a British colonial territory, while he himself was looking into the question whether any might be sent to the British Zone of Germany. Some of these Jews had in fact come from the United States Zone, and it might be possible to arrange for their return there. He had not yet been able to reach definite conclusions, and he proposed to consult with the Prime Minister before a decision was finally taken. No harm would be done by leaving the three transports at Port de Bouc for a few days; and there was a possibility that their passengers might decide eventually to go ashore peaceably.

The Cabinet —

Took note of the Foreign Secretary's Statement.

The Secretary of State for the Colonies informed the Cabinet that the High Commissioner for Palestine had not yet been able to confirm or deny the report that two British non-commissioned officers, who had been kidnapped some days previously, had been executed by the Irgun Zvai Leumi.

CAB 128/10 66(47)

20   UNSCOP's view of the Palestinian situation

117   The atmosphere in Palestine today is one of profound tension. In many respects the country is living under a semi-military regime. In the streets of Jerusalem and the other key areas barbed wire defences, road blocks, machine-gun posts and constant armoured car patrols

are routine measures. In areas of doubtful security administration officials and the military forces live within strictly policed security zones and work within fortified and closely-guarded buildings. Freedom of personal movement is liable to severe restriction and the curfew and martial law have become a not uncommon experience. The primary purpose of the Palestine Government, in the circumstances of recurring terrorist attacks, is to maintain what it regards as the essential conditions of public security. Increasing resort has been had to special security measures provided for in the defence emergency regulations. . . . Under the regulations widespread arrests have been made; and as of 12 July 1947, 820 persons were held in detention on security grounds, including 291 in Kenya under Kenya's 1947 ordinance dealing with the control of detained persons. The detainees were all Jews with the exception of four Arabs. In addition to these, 17,873 illegal immigrants were held under detention.

118   The attitude of the Administration to the maintenance of public security in present circumstances was stated to the Committee in the following terms:

'The right of any community to use force as a means of gaining its political ends is not admitted in the British Commonwealth. Since the beginning of 1945 the Jews have implicitly claimed this right and have supported by an organized campaign of lawlessness, murder and sabotage their contention that, whatever other interests might be concerned, nothing should be allowed to stand in the way of a Jewish State and free Jewish immigration into Palestine. It is true that large numbers of Jews do not today attempt to defend the crimes that have been committed in the name of these political aspirations. They recognize the damage caused to their good name by these methods in the court of world opinion. Nevertheless, the Jewish community of Palestine still publicly refuses its help to the Administration in suppressing terrorism, on the ground that the Administration's policy is opposed to Jewish interests. The converse of this attitude is clear, and its result, however much the Jewish leaders themselves may not wish it, has been to give active encouragement to the dissidents and freer scope to their activities.'

119   There can be no doubt that the enforcement of the White Paper of 1939, subject to the permitted entry since December 1945 of 1,500 Jewish immigrants monthly, has created throughout the Jewish community a deep-seated distrust and resentment against the mandatory Power. This feeling is most sharply expressed in regard to

the Administration's attempts to prevent the landing of illegal immigrants. During its stay in Palestine, the Committee heard from certain of its members an eye-witness account of the incidents relative to the bringing into the port of Haifa, under British naval escort, of the illegal immigrant ship, *Exodus 1947*. In this, as in similar incidents, the Committee has noted the persistence of the attempts to bring Jewish immigrants to Palestine irrespective of determined preventative measures on the part of the Administration, and also the far-reaching support which such attempts receive from the Jewish community in Palestine and abroad. The unremitting struggle to admit further Jews into Palestine, irrespective of the quota permitted by the Administration, is a measure of the rift which has developed between the Jewish Agency and the Jewish community, on the one hand, and the Administration on the other. In the present state of tension, little practicable basis exists for the discharge by the Jewish Agency of its function under the Mandate of 'advising and cooperating' with the Administration in matters affecting the interests of the Jewish community.

120   As far as the Arab community is concerned, the Committee has had less opportunity of ascertaining its attitude in detail in view of the boycott on association with the Committee pronounced by the Arab Higher Committee. During the hearings of representatives of the Arab States at Beirut, however, the Arab assessment of the present situation of unrest in Palestine was stated thus:

'Zionism, however, does not content itself with mere propaganda in favour of the fulfilment of its expansionist projects at the expense of the Arab countries. Its plan involves recourse to terrorism, both in Palestine and in other countries. It is known that a secret army has been formed with a view to creating an atmosphere of tension and unrest by making attempts on the lives of representatives of the governing authority and destroying public buildings. . . . This aggressive attitude, resulting from the mandatory Power's weakness in dealing with them, will not fail to give rise in turn to the creation of similar organizations by the Arabs. The responsibility for the disturbances which might result therefrom throughout the Middle East will rest solely with the Zionist organization, as having been the first to use these violent tactics.' It was declared at the same meeting that 'against a State established by violence, the Arab States will be obliged to use violence; that is a legitimate right of self defence.'

UNSCOP *Report*, vol. 1, chapter II, C
Palestine under the Mandate

21 UNSCOP's plan of partition with economic union

1 The basic premise underlying the partition proposal is that the claims to Palestine of the Arabs and Jews, both possessing validity, are irreconcilable, and that among all the solutions advanced, partition will provide the most realistic and practicable settlement, and is the most likely to afford a workable basis for meeting in part the claims and national aspirations of both parties.

2 It is a fact that both of these peoples have their historic roots in Palestine, and that both make vital contributions to the economic and cultural life of the country. The partition solution takes these considerations fully into account.

3 The basic conflict in Palestine is a clash of two intense nationalisms. Regardless of the historical origins of the conflict, the rights and wrongs of the promises and counter-promises, and the international intervention incident to the Mandate, there are now in Palestine some 650,000 Jews and 1,200,000 Arabs who are dissimilar in their ways of living and, for the time being, separated by political interests which render difficult full and effective political cooperation.

4 Only by means of partition can these conflicting national aspirations find substantial expression and qualify both peoples to take their places as independent nations in the international community and in the United Nations.

5 The partition solution provides that finality which is a most urgent need in the solution. Every other proposed solution would tend to induce the two parties to seek modification in their favour by means of persistent pressure. The grant of independence to both States, however, would remove the basis for such efforts.

6 Partition is based on a realistic appraisal of the actual Arab-Jewish relations in Palestine. Full political cooperation would be indispensable to the effective functioning of any single-State scheme, such as the federal State proposal, except in those cases which frankly envisage either an Arab or a Jewish-dominated State.

7 Partition is the only means available by which political and economic responsibility can be placed equally on both Arabs and Jews, with the prospective result that, confronted with responsibility for bearing fully the consequences of their own actions, a new and important element of political amelioration would be introduced. In the proposed federal-State solution, this factor would be lacking.

8 Jewish immigration is the central issue in Palestine today and is the one factor, above all others, that rules out the necessary cooperation

between the Arab and Jewish communities in a single State. The creation of a Jewish State under a partition scheme is the only hope of removing this issue from the arena of conflict.

9   It is recognized that partition has been strongly opposed by Arabs, but it is felt that opposition would be lessened by a solution which definitively fixes the extent of territory to be allotted to the Jews with its implicit limitation on immigration. The fact that the solution carries the sanction of the United Nations involves a finality which should allay Arab fears of further expansion of the Jewish State.

10   In view of the limited area and resources of Palestine, it is essential that, to the extent feasible, and consistent with the creation of two independent States, the economic unity of the country should be preserved. The partition proposal, therefore, is a qualified partition, subject to such measures and limitations as are considered essential to the further economic and social well-being of both States. Since the economic self-interest of each State would be vitally involved, it is believed that the minimum measure of economic unity is possible, where that of political unity is not.

11   Such economic unity requires the creation of an economic association by means of a treaty between the two States. The essential objectives of this association would be a common customs system, a common currency and the maintenence of a country-wide system of transport and communications.

12   The maintenance of existing standards of social services in all parts of Palestine depends partly upon the preservation of economic unity, and this is a main consideration underlying the provisions for an economic union as part of the partition scheme. Partition, however, necessarily changes to some extent the fiscal situation in such a manner that, at any rate during the early years of its existence, a partitioned Arab State in Palestine would have some difficulty in raising sufficient revenue to keep up its present standards of public services.

One of the aims of the economic union, therefore, is to distribute surplus revenue to support such standards. It is recommended that the division of the surplus revenue, after certain charges and percentage of surplus to be paid to the City of Jerusalem are met, should be in equal proportion to the two States. This is an arbitary proportion but it is considered that it would be acceptable, that it has the merit of simplicity and that, being fixed in this manner, it would be less likely to become a matter of immediate controversy. Provisions are suggested whereby this formula is to be reviewed.

13   This division of customs revenue is justified on three grounds: (1) The Jews will have the more economically developed part of the country embracing practically the whole of the citrus-producing area which includes a large number of Arab producers: (2) the Jewish State would, through the customs union, be guaranteed a larger free-trade area for the sale of the products of its industry: (3) it would be to the disadvantage of the Jewish State if the Arab State should be in a financially precarious and poor economic condition.

14   As the Arab State will not be in a position to undertake considerable development expenditure, sympathetic consideration should be given to its claims for assistance from international institutions in the way of loans for expansion of education, public health and other vital social services of a non-self-supporting nature.

15   International financial assistance would also be required for any comprehensive immigration schemes in the interest of both States, and it is to be hoped that constructive work by the Joint Economic Board will be made possible by means of international loans on favourable terms.

RECOMMENDATIONS.

A PARTITION AND INDEPENDENCE.

1   Palestine within its present borders, following a transitional period of two years from 1 September 1947, shall be constituted into an independent Arab State, an independent Jewish State, and the City of Jerusalem, the boundaries of which are respectively described in Parts II and III below.

> UNSCOP *Report*, vol. 1, chapter VI, part I, Plan of partition with economic union

22   Ernest Bevin's statement to the cabinet on British policy towards the UNSCOP proposals, 20 September 1947

The Foreign Secretary said that when the Report of the Special Committee came before the General Assembly the representatives of other countries might be tempted to put forward unworkable proposals, relying on the fact that it would be for His Majesty's Government to implement them. To obviate this, it was essential that the United Kingdom delegate should make the attitude of His Majesty's Government clear from the start. His own view was that there would be grave disadvantages in any decision by His Majesty's Government to undertake the task of carrying out either the recommendations of the Majority Report or any alternative plan of partition which might be proposed, or the recommendations of the Minority Report. He had therefore been reluctantly driven to the conclusion that the right course was for His Majesty's Government to announce their intention to surrender the Mandate and, failing a satisfactory settlement, to plan for an early withdrawal of the British forces and of the British administration from Palestine. He did not wish to express any opposition to the recommendations in either Report, but he was satisfied that, unless His Majesty's Government announced their intention of abandoning the Mandate and of withdrawing from Palestine, there was no prospect of an agreed settlement; and he was not willing that British forces should be used to enforce a settlement which was unacceptable to either the Arabs or the Jews.

CAB 128/10 76(47)

23   United States Department of State memorandum on American policy at the United Nations, 30 September 1947

Basic Considerations

The position taken by the United States Delegation in the General Assembly on the Palestine question should take full account of the following principal factors:

1   The Near Eastern area is of high strategic significance in over-all American policy. Consequently the maintenance of good will toward the United States on the part of the Moslem world is one of the primary goals of American foreign policy.

2   The policy of the United States toward Palestine over the span of the years since the First World War shows a consistent interest in the establishment of a Jewish National Home. The United States has frequently stated its support of large-scale Jewish immigration into Palestine and has indicated that it might look with favor upon some arrangement providing for a partition of Palestine, provided that such an arrangement gave promise of being workable.

3   The position taken by the United States with regard to the report of the Special Committee on Palestine must indicate the confidence of this Government in the United Nations and United States support of the procedures for which, in this case, it assumed a large initiative.

4   The plan for Palestine ultimately recommended by the General

Assembly should be a *United Nations* solution and not a *United States* solution. It is essential that the basic position to be taken by the United States Delegation to the General Assembly with regard to the Palestine report and the specific tactics followed by the Delegation be such that the final recommendation of the General Assembly cannot be labeled 'the American plan'.

5   It is a matter of urgency that the General Assembly should agree at this session upon a definitive solution of the Palestine problem. The only immediate hope of restoring order in Palestine and thus promoting stability in the whole Near East lies in agreement by the United Nations upon a solution which the interested parties cannot expect by agitation and violence to alter.

6   It is essential that any plan for Palestine adopted by the General Assembly be able to command the maximum cooperation of all elements in Palestine.

FRUS 1947,vol. V, pp. 1166 – 70, 501.
BB Palestine/9 – 3047

24   Jamal Bey Husseini, Arab Higher Committee, before the *Ad Hoc* Committee on the Palestinian Question on Palestinian Arab reactions to the UNSCOP proposals, 29 September 1947

The case of the Arabs of Palestine was based on the principles of international justice; it was that of a people which desired to live in undisturbed possession of the country where Providence and history had placed it. The Arabs of Palestine could not understand why their right to live in freedom and peace, and to develop their country in accordance with their traditions, should be questioned and constantly submitted to investigation.

One thing was clear; it was the sacred duty of the Arabs of Palestine to defend their country against all aggression. The Zionists were conducting an aggressive campaign with the object of securing by force a country which was not theirs by birthright. Thus there was self-defence on one side and, on the other, aggression. The *raison d'être* of the United Nations was to assist self-defence against aggression.

The rights and patrimony of the Arabs in Palestine had been the subject of no less than eighteen investigations within twenty-five years, and all to no purpose. Such commissions of inquiry had made recommendations that had either reduced the national and legal rights of the Palestine Arabs or glossed them over. The few recommendations favourable to the Arabs had been ignored by the Mandatory Power. It was hardly strange, therefore, that they should have been unwilling to take part in a nineteenth investigation. It was for that, and for other reasons already communicated to the United Nations, that they had refused to appear before the United Nations Special Committee on Palestine. Mr Husseini assured the Committee, however, of the respect felt by the Arab Higher Committee for the United Nations and emphasized that his Committee looked to it for justice and equity.

The struggle of the Arabs in Palestine had nothing in common with anti-Semitism. The Arab world had been one of the rare havens of refuge for the Jews until the atmosphere of neighbourliness had been poisoned by the Balfour Declaration and the aggressive spirit the latter had engendered in the Jewish community.

The claims of the Zionists had no legal or moral basis. Their case was based on the association of the Jews with Palestine over two thousand years before. On that basis, the Arabs would have better claims to those territories in other parts of the world such as Spain or parts of France, Turkey, Russia or Afghanistan, which they had inhabited in the past.

Mr Husseini disputed three claims of world Jewry. The claim to Palestine based on historical association was a movement on the part of the Ashkenazim, whose forefathers had no connexion with Palestine. The Sephardim, the main descendants of Israel, had mostly denounced Zionism. Secondly, the religious connexion of the Zionists with Palestine, which he noted was shared by Moslems and Christians, gave them no secular claim to the country. Freedom of access to the Holy Places was universally accepted. Thirdly, the Zionists claimed the establishment of a Jewish National Home by virtue of the Balfour Declaration. But the British Government had had no right to dispose of Palestine which it had occupied in the name of the Allies as a liberator and not as a conqueror. The Balfour Declaration was in contradiction with the Covenant of the League of Nations and was an immoral, unjust and illegal promise.

. . .

The solution lay in the Charter of the United Nations, in accordance with which the Arabs of Palestine, who constituted the majority, were entitled to a free and independent State. Mr Husseini welcomed the recent declaration of the representative of the United Kingdom that the Mandate should be terminated and its termination followed by independence and expressed the hope that the British

Government would not on that occasion, as in the past, reverse its decision under Zionist pressure.

Regarding the manner and form of independence for Palestine, it was the view of the Arab Higher Committee that that was a matter for the rightful owners of Palestine to decide. Once Palestine was found to be entitled to independence, the United Nations was not legally competent to decide or to impose the constitutional organization of Palestine, since such action would amount to interference with an internal matter of an independent nation.

The future constitutional organization of Palestine should be based on the following principles: first, establishment on democratic lines of an Arab State comprising all Palestine; secondly, observance of the said Arab State of Palestine of human rights, fundamental freedoms and equality of all persons before the law; thirdly, protection by the Arab State of the legitimate rights and interests of all the minorities; fourthly, guarantee to all of freedom of worship and access to the Holy Places.

In conclusion, Mr Husseini said that he had not commented on the Special Committee's report because the Arab Higher Committee considered that it could not be a basis for discussion. Both schemes proposed in the report were inconsistent with the United Nations Charter and with the Covenant (sic) League of Nations. The Arabs of Palestine were solidly determined to oppose with all the means at their command any scheme which provided for the dissection, segregation or partition of their country or which gave to a minority special and preferential rights or status. Although they fully realized that big Powers could crush such opposition by brute force, the Arabs nevertheless would not be deterred, but would lawfully defend with their life-blood every inch of the soil of their beloved country.

UNO *Ad Hoc* Committee on the
Palestinian Question, Third Meeting

25 **Rabbi Abba Hillel Silver, Jewish Agency for Palestine, before the *Ad Hoc* Committee on the Palestinian Question on Zionist reactions to the UNSCOP proposals, 2 October 1947**

History was not a story out of the *Arabian Nights* and the Arab Higher Committee was indulging in wishful thinking. Its theory that the Jews of Western Europe were descended from a tribe of Khazars in

Russia was a relatively recent invention, politically inspired. He was surprised that the Arabs of Palestine should wish to engage in genealogical research.

He recalled that at the time when the Allies had liberated Palestine, the country had formed part of a province of the Ottoman Empire and there had been no politically distinct Arab nation. The Arabs had held sway over a heterogeneous population between 636 and 1071 AD and later the Seljuks, the Kurds, the Crusaders, the Egyptian Mamelukes and finally the Ottoman Turks — all non-Arab peoples — had conquered the country. But by 636 AD the Jewish people had already had 2,000 years of history behind it, and Jewish civilization, besides giving rise both to Judaism and Christianity, had also brought forth spiritual leaders venerated also by Islam. In contrast to that, Dr Silver quoted the report of the Royal Commission of 1937, which stated that in the twelve centuries and more that had passed since the Arab conquest, Palestine had virtually dropped out of history, and that in the realm of thought, of science or of letters, it had made no contribution to modern civilization.

Palestine owed its very identity to the Jews, losing it with the Jewish dispersion and resuming its role in history only at the time of the Mandate, which had given it a distinct place alongside the Arab world.

.   .   .

Seventeen million Arabs occupied an area of 1,290,000 square miles of great wealth, including all the principal Arab and Moslem centres, while Palestine, after the loss of Transjordan was only 10,000 square miles. The majority plan, set out in chapter VII of the Special Committee's report, proposed that that area should be reduced by one half. The plan, unlike that of the Royal Commission, eliminated western Galilee from the proposed Jewish State: that was an injustice and grievous handicap to the development of the Jewish State.

The majority plan proposed that the City of Jerusalem should be established as a separate unit. But modern Jersualem contained a compact Jewish community of 90,000 inhabitants, and included the central national, religious and educational institutions of the Jewish people of Palestine. Moreover, Jerusalem held a unique place in Jewish life and religious traditions. It was the ancient capital of the Jewish nation and its symbol throughout the ages. 'If I forget thee, O Jerusalem, let my right hand forget her cunning': that was the vow of the Psalmist, and of an exiled people throughout the ages.

Dr Silver strongly urged that the Jewish section of modern

Jerusalem, outside the walls, should be included in the Jewish State. He also reserved the right to deal later with other territorial modifications.

If that heavy sacrifice was the inescapable condition of a final solution, if it made possible the immediate re-establishment of the Jewish State, that ideal for which a people had ceaselessly striven, if it allowed an immediate influx of immigrants, which would be possible only in a Jewish State, then the Jewish Agency was prepared to recommend the acceptance of the partition solution to the supreme organs of the movement, subject to further discussion of constitutional and territorial provisions. That sacrifice would be the Jewish contribution to the solution of a painful problem and would bear witness to the Jewish people's spirit of international cooperation and its desire for peace.

The Jewish Agency accepted the proposal for economic union despite the heavy sacrifices which the Jewish State would have to make in that matter too. It was a promising and statesmanlike conception for, as stated in part I, chapter VI of the Special Committee's report, 'in view of the limited area and resources of Palestine, it is essential that, to the extent feasible, and consistent with the creation of two independent States, the economic unity of the country should be preserved.' The limit to the sacrifices to which the Jewish Agency could consent was clear: a Jewish State must have in its own hands those instruments of financing and economic control necessary to carry out large-scale Jewish immigration and the related economic development, and it must have independent access to those world sources of capital and raw materials indispensable for the accomplishment of those purposes.

The Jews of Palestine wanted to be good neigbours in their relations not only with the Arab State of Palestine but with the other Arab States. They intended to respect the equal rights of the Arab population in the free and democratic Jewish State. What the Jews had already achieved in Palestine augured well for the future. Nevertheless, if that offer of peace and friendship were not welcomed in the same spirit, the Jews would defend their rights to the end. In Palestine there had been built a nation which demanded its independence, and would not allow itself to be dislodged or deprived of its national status. It could not go, and it would not go, beyond the enormous sacrifice which had been asked of it.

UNO *Ad Hoc* Committee on the
Palestinian Question, Fourth Meeting

26   Draft resolution of the Sub-Committee 1 of the *Ad Hoc* Committee on the Palestine Question, 19 November 1947

The General Assembly

.   .   .

Recommends to the United Kingdom, as the Mandatory Power for Palestine, and to all other Members of the United Nations, the adoption and implementation, with regard to the future government of Palestine, of the Plan of Partition with Economic Union set out below;

PLAN OF PARTITION WITH ECONOMIC UNION

PART I: FUTURE CONSTITUTION AND GOVERNMENT OF PALESTINE
A   Termination of Mandate. Partition and Independence.
1   The Mandate for Palestine shall terminate at a date to be agreed on by the commission of five members referred to in paragraph 1 of section B below and the Mandatory Power, with the approval of the Security Council, but in any case not later than 1 August 1948.
2   The armed forces of the Mandatory Power shall be progressively withdrawn from Palestine, the withdrawal to be completed on a date to be agreed by the commission and the Mandatory Power, with the approval of the Security Council, but in any case not later than 1 August 1948.

The Mandatory Power shall advise the commission as far in advance as possible, of its intention to evacuate each area.

The Mandatory Power shall use its best endeavours to ensure that an area situated in the territory of the Jewish State, including a seaport and hinterland adequate to provide facilities for a substantial immigration, shall be evacuated at the earliest date and in any event not later than 1 February 1948.
3   Independent Arab and Jewish States and the special international regime for the City of Jerusalem set forth in part III of this plan, shall come into existence in Palestine two months after the evacuation of the armed forces of the Mandatory Power has been completed but in any case not later than 1 October 1948. The boundaries of the Arab State, the Jewish State and the City of Jerusalem shall be as described in parts II and III below.
4   The period between the adoption by the General Assembly of its recommendation on the question of Palestine and the establishment of

the independence of the Arab and Jewish States shall be a transitional period.

B   *Steps Preparatory to Independence.*

1   There shall be a commission appointed by the General Assembly of five members, representing Guatemala, Iceland, Norway, Poland and Uruguay.

2   The administration of Palestine during the transitional period shall be entrusted to the commission, which shall act in conformity with the recommendations of the General Assembly, under the guidance of the Security Council.

In the discharge of this administrative responsibility, the commission shall have authority to issue necessary regulations and take other measures as required.

The Mandatory Power shall not issue any regulations to prevent, obstruct or delay the implementation by the commission of the measures recommended by the General Assembly.

3   On its arrival in Palestine, the commission shall proceed to carry out measures for the establishment of the frontiers of the Arab and Jewish States and the City of Jerusalem in accordance with the recommendations of the General Assembly on the partition of Palestine.

4   The commission, after consultation with the democratic parties and other public organizations of the Arab and Jewish States, shall select and establish in each State as rapidly as possible a provisional council of Government. The activities of both the Arab and Jewish provisional councils of government shall be carried out under the general direction of the commission.

D.   *Economic Union and Transit.*

1   The provisional council of government of each State shall enter into an undertaking with respect to economic union and transit. This undertaking shall be drafted by the commission provided for in section B, paragraph 1, utilizing to the greatest possible extent the advice and cooperation of representative organizations and bodies from each of the proposed States. It shall contain provisions to establish the economic union of Palestine and provide for other matters of common interest. If by 1 April 1948 the provisional councils of government have not entered into the undertaking, the undertaking shall be put into force by the commission.

The economic union of Palestine.

2   The objectives of the economic union of Palestine shall be:

(a) A customs union;

(b) A joint currency system providing for a single foreign exchange rate;

(c) Operation in the common interest, on a non-discriminatory basis, of railways, inter-State highways, postal, telephone, and telegraphic services, and ports and airports involved in international trade and commerce;

(d) Access for both States and for the City of Jerusalem, on a non-discriminatory basis, to water and power facilities.

3   There shall be established a joint economic board, which shall consist of three representatives of each of the two States and three foreign members appointed by the Economic and Social Council of the United Nations. The foreign members shall be appointed in the first instance for a term of three years: they shall serve as individuals and not as representatives of States.

4   The functions of the joint economic board shall be to implement either directly or by delegation the measures necessary to realize the objectives of the economic union. It shall have all the powers of organization and administration necessary to fulfil its functions.

.   .   .

PART III: *CITY OF JERUSALEM.*

A Special Regime.

The City of Jerusalem shall be established as a *corpus separatum* under a special international regime and shall be administered by the United Nations. The Trusteeship Council shall be designated to discharge the responsibilities of the Administering Authority on behalf of the United Nations.

> UNO Report of Sub-Committee 1 of the *Ad Hoc* Committee on the Palestinian Question, Doc. A/AC. 14/34 and Corr. 1 and Add. 1.

27 Speech by Sir Alexander Cadogan, United Kingdom, before the *Ad Hoc* Committee on the Palestinian Question, 20 November 1947

Sir Alexander Cadogan (United Kingdom) regretted that no progress had been possible in the direction of conciliation between the two peoples most directly concerned with the future of Palestine. The absence of that conciliation created exceptional difficulty since it could hardly be imagined that the proposals of Sub-Committee 1 should be acceptable to the Arab population, or that the proposals of Sub-Committee 2 would be acceptable to the Jewish population of Palestine.

.   .   .

The limits within which the United Kingdom Government was prepared to participate in giving effect to any settlement which failed to win approval of both Arabs and Jews in Palestine had been clearly stated in the 2nd and 15th meetings. The United Kingdom could not deviate from these principles: it could not play a major part in the implementation of a scheme which was not acceptable to both Arabs and Jews, but it would not wish to impede the implementation of a recommendation of the General Assembly. The United Kingdom Government had assumed that the General Assembly would take account of the risk of strife in Palestine and of the need to provide means of filling the gap left by the decision of the Mandatory Power that its troops should not be used to enforce the decision of the United Nations. Sir Alexander felt bound, however, to make clear the extent to which the role assigned to his Government by Sub-Committee 1 was compatible with the declared intentions of his Government.

According to the definition of the period of transition laid down in paragraph 4 of Part I(A) of the Sub-Committee's plan that period would commence within a few days. It followed that the United Kingdom Government would continue to hold the Mandate for Palestine. However, in paragraph 2 of Part I(B) the Sub-Committee proposed that the administration of Palestine during the transitional period should be entrusted to a United Nations commission. No better way could be found of creating confusion and disorder in Palestine than by the establishment of an authority which would operate concurrently with the existing mandatory administration. It must be made clear that the United Kingdom Government would insist upon its undivided control of Palestine as long as it continued to hold the Mandate.

> UNO *Ad Hoc* Committee on the
> Palestinian Question, Twenty-Fifth
> Meeting

28 The amended version of the *Ad Hoc* Committee's resolution, 21 November 1947

The *Ad Hoc* Committee on the Palestinian Question, at its 25th meeting on 20 November 1947, decided that Sub-Committee 1 should meet to consider any alterations in its recommendations that might be necessary in the light of the statement which had just been made to the *Ad Hoc* Committee by the representative of the United Kingdom.

Sub-Committee 1 recommends to the *Ad Hoc* Committee the adoption of the draft resolution and plan as amended.

AMENDMENTS TO PART I (A)

1   The Mandate for Palestine shall terminate *as soon as possible* but in any case not later than 1 August 1948.
2   The armed forces of the Mandatory Power shall be progressively withdrawn from Palestine, the withdrawal to be completed *as soon as possible* but in any case not later than 1 August 1948.

The Mandatory Power shall advise the commission, as far in advance as possible, of its intention *to terminate the Mandate* and to evacuate each area.

The Mandatory Power shall use its best endeavours to ensure that an area situated in the territory of the Jewish State; including a seaport and hinterland adequate to provide facilities for a substantial immigration, shall be evacuated at the earliest possible date and in any event not later than 1 February 1948.

AMENDMENTS TO PART I (B)

2   The administration of Palestine shall, *as the Mandatory Power withdraws its armed forces, be progressively turned over* to the commission which shall act in conformity with the recommendations of the General Assembly, under the guidance of the Seccurity Council. *The Mandatory Power shall to the fullest possible extent coordinate its plans for withdrawal with the plans of the commission to take over and administer areas which have been evacuated.*

In the discharge of this administrative responsibility the commission shall have authority to issue necessary regulations and other measures as required.

The Mandatory Power shall not *take any action* to prevent, obstruct or delay the implementation by the commission of the measures recommended by the General Assembly.

> UNO Additional report of Sub-Committee 1 to the *Ad Hoc* Committee on the Palestinian Question, Doc. A/AC. 14/34 /Add. 2

29 Speech by Mahmoud Bey Fawzi, Egypt, before the General Assembly of the United Nations, 26 November 1947

We have been told about the situation in which one of the great Powers finds itself, about the predicament in which it thinks, òr perhaps feels, that it is entangled. We have been told concerning that great Power, that being confronted with the imminence of a general national election, its candidates seek the vote of a single component state, and that vote depends on the Jewish electorate of a single city. Thus is its policy dictated with regard to a Palestine which is more than five thousand miles away. That is what we have been told. We do not wish to believe it; we wish to hope it is not true.

If the General Assembly's resolution is passed, I must reiterate that we shall take it for what it is: a mere recommendation addressed to the Egyptian Government. I must, in terms of no equivocation, reiterate our position as it has been stated throughout the deliberations of the *Ad Hoc* Committee on the Palestinian Question. This position is:

1 We are of the opinion that the General Assembly is not competent to make the proposed recommendation to Egypt or to any other State;

2 In view of the difference of opinion on this question of competence, we requested, more than forty days ago, that the General Assembly should ask the International Court of Justice for an advisory opinion. We would still like to be enlightened by such an opinion from the Court;

3 Failing an advisory opinion of the International Court of Justice, Egypt will be guided only by its own views as to the powers conferred on the General Assembly by the Charter;

4 As at present advised, we will not adopt and we will not implement the proposed recommendation by the General Assembly if it obtains the necessary vote and is adopted;

5 As a sovereign, equal Member of the United Nations, Egypt reserves its full rights under the Charter.

> UNO GAOR, 2nd Session, 1947, Hundred and Twenty-Fourth Plenary

Meeting, 123, Palestinian question:
report of the *Ad Hoc* Committee on the
Palestinian Question

30 Speech by Andrei Gromyko, USSR, before the General Assembly of the United Nations, 26 November 1947

We may ask why it is that the overwhelming majority of the delegations represented in the General Assembly adopted this solution and not another. The only explanation that can be given is that all the alternative solutions of the Palestinian problem were found to be unworkable and impractical. In stating this, I have in mind the project of creating a single independent Arab-Jewish State with equal rights for Arabs and Jews. The experience gained from study of the Palestinian question, including the experience of the Special Committee, has shown that Jews and Arabs in Palestine do not wish or are unable to live together. The logical conclusion followed that, if these two peoples that inhabit Palestine, both of which have deeply rooted historical ties with the land, cannot live together within the boundaries of a single State, there is no alternative but to create, in place of one country, two States — an Arab and a Jewish one. It is, in the view of our delegation, the only workable solution.

The representatives of the Arab States claim that the partition of Palestine would be an historic injustice. But this view of the case is unacceptable, if only because, after all, the Jewish people has been closely linked with Palestine for a considerable period in history. Apart from that, we must not overlook — and the USSR delegation drew attention to this circumstance originally at the special session of the General Assembly — we must not overlook the position in which the Jewish people found themselves as a result of the recent world war. I shall not repeat what the USSR delegation said on this point at the special session of the General Assembly. However, it may not be amiss to remind my listeners again that, as a result of the war which was unleashed by Hitlerite Germany, the Jews, as a people, have suffered more than any other people. You know that there was not a single country in Western Europe which succeeded in adequately protecting the interests of the Jewish people against the arbitary acts and violence of the Hitlerites.

UNO GAOR, 2nd Session, 1947, Hun-

dred and Twenty-Fifth Plenary Meeting,
124, Continuation of the discussion on
the Palestinian question

31 Memorandum by the Acting Secretary of State to President Truman, 10 December 1947

Ambassador O'Neal at Manila has asked that you be informed of a conversation which he had on 30 November 1947 with President Roxas concerning the Philippine vote in the United Nations on the Palestine partition question.

As you will recall, the Philippine Delegate to the United Nations, Ambassador Romulo, in an address before the General Assembly of the United Nations on 26 November 1947, indicated that the Philippines would vote against Palestine partition. When the vote was taken, however, on 29 November the Philippines voted in favor of partition.

In his telegram, Ambassador O'Neal reports that President Roxas stated that he had instructed the Philippine Delegation to change its position and vote in favor of partition because of his fear, based on a report from Ambassador Elizalde and a telegram from some ten United States Senators, that a vote against partition would have an adverse effect on United States-Philippine relations.

FRUS 1947, vol. 5, pp. 1305 – 6, 501.
BB Palestine/12 – 1047

32 Memorandum by President Truman to the Acting Secretary of State, 11 December 1947.

I read with a lot of interest your memorandum of the tenth in regard to the Philippine situation.

It seems to me that if our Delegation to the United Nations is to be interfered with by members of the United States Senate and by pressure groups in this country we will be helping the United Nations down the road to failure.

The conversation between the President of the Philippines and our Ambassador is most interesting.

I have a report from Haiti, in which it is said that our Consul in Haiti approached the President of that country and suggested to him that for his own good he should order the vote of his country changed, claiming that he had instructions from me to make such a statement to the President of Haiti. As you very well know, I refused to make any statements to any country on the subject of its vote in the United Nations.

It is perfectly apparent that pressure groups will succeed in putting the United Nations out of business if this sort of thing is continued and I am anxious that it be stopped.

FRUS 1947, vol. 5, p. 1309,
501/12 – 1147

33   Report of the United Nations Palestine Commission, 10 April 1948

2   The Jewish Agency for Palestine cooperated with the Commission in its task of implementing the Assembly's resolution. The Governments of the Arab States and the Arab Higher Committee not only withheld their cooperation from the Commission, but actively opposed the Assembly's resolution. As the Commission reported to the Security Council in its first Special Report (S/676) on 16 February 1948, 'Powerful Arab interests, both inside and outside Palestine, are defying the resolution of the General Assembly and are engaged in a deliberate effort to alter by force the settlement envisaged therein.' Armed Arab bands from neighbouring Arab States have infiltrated into the territory of Palestine and together with local Arab forces are defeating the purposes of the resolution by acts of violence. The Jews, on the other hand, are determined to ensure the establishment of the Jewish State, as envisaged by the resolution. The resulting conditions of insecurity in Palestine have made it impossible for the Commission to implement the Assembly's resolution without the assistance of adequate armed forces.

3   The policy of the Mandatory Power, and particularly its refusal to take any measure which might be construed as involving it in the implementation of the Assembly's resolution, has had the following consequences:

(a) The provisions of the Assembly's resolution for a progressive transfer of administration from the mandatory Power to the Commission have not been complied with. The mandatory Power has insisted on retaining undivided control of Palestine until the date of termination of the Mandate and on relinquishing the whole complex of governmental responsibilities on that day, except for the areas still occupied by British troops. In the view of the mandatory Power the progressive transfer of authority refers only to those areas.

(b) The Commission could not proceed to Palestine until two weeks prior to the termination of the Mandate. The insistence of the mandatory Power on this point, even though the Commission has been prepared to restrict its activities in Palestine prior to 15 May 1948, to preparatory work and would not attempt to exercise any authority there, made it impossible for the Commission to take the necessary preparatory measures to ensure continuity in administration after the date of termination of the Mandate.

(c) The Commission could not take any measures to establish the frontiers of the Arab and Jewish States and the City of Jerusalem, since the mandatory Power informed the Commission that it could not facilitate the delimitation of frontiers on the ground.

(d) The refusal of the mandatory Power to permit any Provisional Council of Government, whether Arab or Jewish, if selected, to carry out any functions prior to the termination of the Mandate, made it necessary for the Commission, in accordance with part I.B.4 of the resolution of the General Assembly, to communicate that fact to the Security Council and to the Secretary-General.

(e) The refusal of the mandatory Power to permit the taking of preparatory steps towards the establishment of the armed militia, envisaged by the resolution for the purpose of maintaining internal order and preventing frontier clashes, has made it impossible to implement the Assembly's resolution in that respect.

. . .

5   The Commission, therefore, has the duty to report to the General Assembly that the armed hostility of both Palestinian and non-Palestinian Arab elements, the lack of cooperation from the mandatory Power, the disintegrating security situation in Palestine, and the fact that the Security Council did not furnish the Commission with the necessary armed assistance, are the factors which have made it impossible for the Commission to implement the Assembly's resolution.

> UNO GAOR, 2nd Special Session, Supplement No. 1, *Report of the UN Palestine Commission*, chapter VI, Conclusions

34   The American Consul at Jerusalem to the Secretary of State, 13
     April 1948

Early morning 9 April combined force Irgun and Stern Gang
numbering over 100 attacked Arab village, Deir Yassin, several miles
west Jerusalem. Attackers killed 250 persons of whom half, by their
own admission to American correspondents, were women and
children. Attacks carried out in connection battle now still in progress
between Arabs Jews on roads leading to Jerusalem from Tel Aviv.

Arab reaction to attack has been violent and emotions, already at
high pitch following death 8 April of Abdul Kader Husseini (Arab
Jerusalem commander) during Arab attempt retake village captured
by Haganah, now at bursting point. Officer ConGen visiting Hussein
Khalidi, secretary Arab Higher Executive, 11 April found him still
trembling with rage and emotion and referring to attack as 'worst Nazi
tactic'.

As indignation, resentment and determination to avenge Deir
Yassin spread among Arabs, we believe, chance for cease-fire and
truce increasingly remote. With growing criticism in Irgun and Stern
Gang circles over Haganah leadership further attacks this nature can
be expected and Arabs will react violently.

                         FRUS 1948, vol. 5, part 2, p. 817, 867N.
                         01/4 – 1348

IV

The Creation of the State of Israel and the First Arab-Israeli War

With the departure of the British High Commissioner on 14 May 1948, the State of Israel was proclaimed (35), being accorded immediate *de facto* recognition by the United States. The following day, the first Arab-Israeli war commenced when troops from Egypt, Transjordan, Syria, Iraq and Lebanon attacked Israeli positions (36), justifying their action in terms of standing by their avowed aim of creating a unitary Palestinian state. On 14 May, in an attempt to resolve the impending crisis, the General Assembly had appointed as its Mediator the Swedish diplomat, Count Folke Bernadotte. Under his auspices, a truce was arranged from 11 June to 9 July, followed by another from 18 July. Document 37 gives the American Central Intelligence Agency's appraisal of how the war was developing in Israel's favour at this point, explaining the nature of the fighting and their estimate of the forces involved. Bernadotte's sombre view of the complex and frustrating political situation which had been created is revealed in document 38. By 16 September, he had formulated his proposals for a permanent solution (39), but the following day he was assassinated by Sternists in Jerusalem. Fighting continued until early January 1949 when, under the aegis of the United Nations, negotiations for an Egyptian-Israeli armistice were held at Rhodes, an agreement being signed there on 24 February (40). Similar agreements were concluded with Lebanon on 23 March, Jordan on 3 April, and Syria on 20 July. Not only had Israel survived the war but she had done so with territories considerably larger than those encompassed by the United Nations resolution (**Map 2**). The Palestinians, with their supporters in the Arab world, had seen the collapse of their aspirations for a unitary independent state without even the consolation of the Arab state in a partitioned Palestine which the United Nations proposals had always envisaged. The Gaza strip passed under Egyptian administration, while east Jerusalem and the other fragment of the proposed Palestinian Arab state on the west bank of the river Jordan were formally annexed by

King Abdullah of Jordan in April 1950, despite opposition in the Arab League. By then, three-quarters of a million Palestinian Arabs had become refugees in circumstances of considerable controversy (41).

35   Declaration of the establishment of the State of Israel, 14 May 1948

Eretz-Israel[1] was the birthplace of the Jewish people. Here their spiritual, religious and political identity was shaped. Here they first attained to statehood, created cultural values of national and universal significance and gave to the world the eternal Book of Books.

After being forcibly exiled from their land, the people kept faith with it throughout their dispersion and never ceased to pray and hope for their return to it and for the restoration in it of their political freedom.

Impelled by this historic and traditional attachment, Jews strove in every successive generation to re-establish themselves in their ancient homeland. In recent decades they returned in their masses. Pioneers, Ma'apilim[2] and defenders, they made deserts bloom, revived the Hebrew language, built villages and towns, and created a thriving community, controlling its own economy and culture, loving peace but knowing how to defend itself, bringing the blessings of progress to all the country's inhabitants, and aspiring towards independent nationhood.

In the year 5657 (1897), at the summons of the spiritual father of the Jewish state, Theodor Herzl, the first Zionist Congress convened and proclaimed the right of the Jewish people to national rebirth in their own country.

This right was recognized in the Balfour Declaration of 2 November, 1917, and reaffirmed in the Mandate of the League of Nations which, in particular, gave international sanction to the historic connection between the Jewish people and Eretz-Israel and to the right of the Jewish people to rebuild its national home.

The catastrophe which recently befell the Jewish people – the massacre of millions of Jews in Europe – was another clear demostration of the urgency of solving the problem of its homelessness by re-establishing in Eretz-Israel the Jewish state, which would open the gates of the homeland wide to every Jew and confer upon the Jewish

1   The land of Israel, Palestine.
2   Immigrants who had come in defiance of British policy.

people the status of a fully-privileged member of the comity of nations.

Survivors of the Nazi holocaust in Europe, as well as Jews from other parts of the world, continued to migrate to Eretz-Israel, undaunted by the difficulties, restrictions and dangers, and never ceased to assert their right to a life of dignity, freedom and honest toil in their national homeland.

In the second world ·· ar, the Jewish community of this country contributed its full share to the struggle of the freedom — and peace-loving nations against the forces of Nazi wickedness and, by the blood of its soldiers and its war effort, gained the right to be reckoned among the peoples who founded the United Nations.

On 29 November, 1947, the United Nations General Assembly passed a resolution calling for the establishment of a Jewish state in Eretz-Israel; the General Assembly required the inhabitants of Eretz-Israel to take such steps as were necessary on their part for the implementation of that resolution. This recognition by the United Nations of the right of the Jewish people to establish their state is irrevocable.

This right is the natural right of the Jewish people to be masters of their own fate, like all other nations, in their own sovereign state.

Accordingly we, members of the People's Council, representatives of the Jewish community of Eretz-Israel and of the Zionist movement, are here assembled on the day of the termination of the British Mandate over Eretz-Israel and, by virtue of our natural and historic right and on the strength of the resolution of the United Nations General Assembly, hereby declare the establishment of a Jewish state in Eretz-Israel, to be known as the State of Israel.

We declare that, with effect from the moment of the termination of the Mandate, being tonight, the eve of Sabbath, the 6th Iyar, 5708 (15 May 1948), until the establishment of the elected, regular authorities of the state in accordance with the constitution which shall be adopted by the elected Constituent Assembly not later than 1 October 1948, the People's Council shall act as a provisional Council of State, and its executive organ, the People's Administration, shall be the Provisional Government of the Jewish state, to be called 'Israel'.

The State of Israel will be open for Jewish immigration and for the ingathering of the exiles; it will foster the development of the country for the benefit of all its inhabitants; it will be based on freedom, justice and peace as envisaged by the Prophets of Israel; it will ensure complete equality of social and political rights to all its inhabitants irrespective of religion, race or sex; it will guarantee freedom of religion, conscience, language, education and culture; it will safe-guard the Holy Places of all religions; and it will be faithful to the prin-ciples of the Charter of the United Nations.

The State of Israel is prepared to cooperate with the agencies and representatives of the United Nations in implementing the resolution of the General Assembly of 29 November 1947, and will take steps to bring about the economic union of the whole of Eretz-Israel.

We appeal to the United Nations to assist the Jewish people in the building-up of its state and to receive the State of Israel into the comity of nations.

We appeal—in the very midst of the onslaught launched against us now for months—to the Arab inhabitants of the State of Israel to preserve peace and participate in the upbuilding of the state on the basis of full and equal citizenship and due representation in all its provisional and permanent institutions.

We extend our hand to all neighbouring states and their peoples in an offer of peace and good neighbourliness, and appeal to them to establish bonds of cooperation and mutual help with the sovereign Jewish people settled in its own land. The State of Israel is prepared to do its share in a common effort for the advancement of the entire Middle East.

We appeal to the Jewish people throughout the Diaspora[3] to rally round the Jews of Eretz-Israel in the tasks of immigration and upbuilding and to stand by them in the great struggle for the realiza-tion of the age-old dream—the redemption of Israel.

Placing our trust in the Almighty, we affix our signatures to this proclamation at this session of the Provisional Council of State, on the soil of the homeland, in the city of Tel Aviv, on this Sabbath eve, the 5th day of Iyar 5708 (14 May 1948).

Israel Information Service

36   Cablegram from the Secretary-General of the League of Arab States to the Secretary-General of the United Nations, 15 May 1948

On the occasion of the intervention of Arab States in Palestine to restore law and order and to prevent disturbances prevailing in Palestine from spreading into their territories and to check further bloodshed, I have the honour to request your Excellency to bring

3   The Dispersion.

following statement before General Assembly and Security Council.

Now that the Mandate over Palestine has come to an end, leaving no legally constituted authority behind in order to administer law and order in the country and afford the necessary and adequate protection to life and property, the Arab States declare as follows:

(a) The right to set up a Government in Palestine pertains to its inhabitants under the principles of self-determination recognized by the Covenant of the League of Nations as well as the United Nations Charter;

(b) Peace and order have been completely upset in Palestine, and, in consequence of Jewish aggression, approximately over a quarter of a million of the Arab population have been compelled to leave their homes and emigrate to neighbouring Arab countries. The prevailing events in Palestine exposed the concealed aggressive intentions of the Zionists and the imperialistic motives, as clearly shown in their acts committed upon those peaceful Arabs and villages of Deer Yasheen, Tiberias, and other places, as well as by their encroachment upon the building and bodies of the inviolable consular codes, manifested by their attack upon the Consulate in Jerusalem.

(c) The Mandatory has already announced that on the termination of the Mandate it will no longer be responsible for maintenance of law and order in Palestine except in the camps and areas actually occupied by its forces, and only to the extent necessary for the security of these forces and their withdrawal. This leaves Palestine absolutely without any administrative authority entitled to maintain, and capable of maintaining, a machinery of administration of the country adequate for the purpose of ensuring due protection of life and property. There is further the threat that this lawlessness may spread to the neighbouring Arab States where feeling is already tense on account of the prevailing conditions in Palestine. The respective members of the Arab League, and as Members of the United Nations at the same time, feel gravely perturbed and deeply concerned over this situation.

.   .   .

The Governments of the Arab States hereby confirm at this stage the view that had been repeatedly declared by them on previous occasions, such as the London Conference and before the United Nations mainly (sic), the only fair and just solution to the problem of Palestine is the creation of a United State of Palestine based upon the democratic principles which will enable all its inhabitants to enjoy equality before the law, and which would guarantee to all minorities the safeguards provided for in all democratic constitutional States affording at the same time full protection and free access to Holy Places. The Arab States emphatically and repeatedly declare that their intervention in Palestine has been prompted solely by the considerations and for the aims set out above and that they are not inspired by any other motive whatsoever. They are, therefore, confident that their action will receive the support of the United Nations as tending to further the aims and ideals of the United Nations as set out in its Charter.

> UNO SCOR, Third Year, Supplement for May 1948, doc. S/745

37 Report by the American Central Intelligence Agency, 'Possible Developments from the Palestine Truce', 27 July 1948

The Military Situation in Palestine at the Beginning of the Second Truce – 18 July 1948.

The military situation on 18 July, the beginning of the second truce in Palestine, shows that the Jews have made substantial gains during the nine-day period of fighting between 9 July and 18 July. During that period the Jews captured Lydda, Ramle, and Ras el Zin, thereby removing the danger of an Arab thrust on Tel-Aviv. In the north they took the strategic Arab-Christian town of Nazareth and consolidated their positions along the Lebanese border into which units had been moved during the truce. In the south the Jews thrust southeast into the Egyptian-occupied area near Isdud and widened and strengthened the strip to Jewish-controlled territory along the roads between Jerusalem and Tel-Aviv. The only successful Arab action during that period, the Iraqi advance north from Jenin towards Afule, was halted by the truce before any significant gains were made.

During the period of the truce the Jews gained considerably from a military point of view. They strengthened and improved their existing fortifications and built new ones in the areas recently taken over from the Arabs. They improved the by-pass road to Jerusalem, which skirts Arab-held Latrun and Bab el Wad on the main road from Jerusalem to Tel-Aviv. They recruited and trained troops both abroad and in Palestine, and reinforcements were flown in from abroad. They increased their supply of tanks, aeroplanes and artillery. The Jews brought heavy artillery into the Jerusalem area and are reported to have acquired at least 13 German ME – 109 fighter planes – which can be converted into light bombers – and 3 B – 17's. (They are now reported to possess a total of 60 ME – 109's, of which 24 are operational.) The food situation in Jerusalem was greatly improved during the truce.

The Arabs made certain gains during the truce, but these were insignificant compared with the Jewish gains. The Arabs received some Italian and Belgian arms and brought more arms and ammunition to the front.

The truce resulted in so great an improvement in the Jewish capabilities that the Jews may now be strong enough to launch a full-scale offensive and drive the Arab forces out of Palestine. Events during the truce, and the enormous increase in Jewish strength resulting from them, considerably change the previously held estimate of the probable course of the war in Palestine. The Arabs' logistical position generally is very bad and their ammunition supply is exceedingly low. It is estimated that they could not continue to fight, even on the previous moderate scale, for more than two to three months.

The Military Forces involved are estimated as:

Arab Forces in or near Palestine.

Army	In Palestine	Near Palestine	Total
Transjordan	6,000	4,000	10,000
Iraq	9,000	1,000	10,000
Egypt	5,000	8,000	13,000
Syria	1,000	1,500	2,500
Lebanon		1,800	1,800
Saudi Arabia	3,000(?)		3,000
Irregulars	3,000(?)	3,500	6,500
Totals	27,000	19,800	46,800

Israeli Forces

Haganah
Mobile Striking Force	17,000
Semi-Mobile Force (Local operation)	18,000
Garrison or Defense (settlers-urban militia)	50,000

Irgun Zvai Leumi

The Irgun has gradually increased from 7,000 to 12,000 during the past 4 to 6 months.

Stern Gang

A similar rise in Stern Gang numbers from 400 – 800 has been recently confirmed.

Total   97,800

FRUS 1948, vol. 5, part 2, pp. 1240 – 8, CIA Files

38 The American Chargé in Egypt to the Secretary of State on Count Bernadotte's mission, 7 August 1948.

1   Count Bernadotte in reviewing recent developments his mission Palestine with Ireland at Alexandria said he was making progress in obtaining acquiescence existence Israeli state if not its formal acceptance by Arab states. His talks with Transjordan and Lebanese Prime Ministers indicated Transjordan and Lebanon would so acquiesce. Both sought speedy decision. Azzam Pasha[1] also apparently convinced necessity to admit existence Jewish state although not ready to make statement now since he believed time should be given for preparation public opinion. Bernadotte had pointed out to Azzam Pasha that decision could not be delayed beyond next meeting GA in September. Bernadotte expected to see Prime Minister Nokrashy Pasha[2] for his views this problem and that of refugees. He had not seen Prime Ministers Syria or Iraq but expected them to be more intransigent.

2   With reference refugees Bernadotte said condition 300,000 to 400,000 Arab refugees without food, clothing and shelter was appalling. He hoped various welfare organizations could be induced to take interest but basic problem was their eventual return to their home. In this connection Bernadotte said PGI[3] was 'showing signs of swelled-head'. Shertok[4] to whom he had put this most pressing and urgent problem had indicated politically PGI could not admit Arab refugees as they would constitute fifth-column. Economically PGI had no room for Arabs since their space was needed for Jewish immigrants. Shertok when pressed had replied that nothing could be done until

1   Secretary-General of the Arab League.
2   Prime Minister of Egypt, assassinated 28 December 1948.
3   Provisional Government of Israel.
4   Moshe Sharett (Shertok), Israeli Foreign Minister and later Prime Minister.

peace was made. In any event government reserved right to replace them with Jews from Arab countries who had expressed desire to come to Palestine. Bernadotte commented that it seemed anomaly for Jews to base demand for Jewish state on need to find home Jewish refugees and that they should demand migration to Palestine of Jewish DP's when they refused to recognize problem of Arab refugees which they had created.

In regard to property Arab refugees he said apparently most had been seized for use by Jews. He had seen Haganah organizing and supervising removal contents Arab houses in Ramle which he understood was being distributed among newly arrived Jewish immigrants. He was also putting problem before SC but was not counting on its assistance. He also spoke of asking for special session GA to consider refugees.

3 Concerning future peace Palestine he would put forward no further proposals but would engage in informal talks. In addition to necessity acknowledging existence Jewish state three possibilities lay before Arabs (1) resumption of war, (2) creation of Arab state as proposed in November 29 SC (sic) resolution, (3) partition of Arab Palestine among Arab states. Apparently he leaned towards last solution as enabling Arab states to publicize definite benefits to their people.

He was also working for consolidation Israeli territory although PGI was proving completely intractable. It demanded retention of all Galilee by right of conquest, corridor from Jerusalem to Tel Aviv, and the return of Negeb as an area promised Israel in partition scheme. He commented that role of peacemaker for Palestine was decidedly no easy one.

4 Bernadotte indicated great concern for immediate future Jerusalem. Was convinced action was brewing there. He had called attention [of] Bernard Joseph, Military Governor Jerusalem to alleged statement by Shertok that Jews now had right to fight Egyptians everywhere since they had attacked Jews in Negeb. He had informed Joseph this was contrary to fact and he hoped Shertok would withdraw statement. Joseph said he could not agree with Bernadotte's views. Bernadotte said he would raise question with Shertok when he saw him 5 August.

5 He expressed concern that UN was not giving him tools required for task including adequate observers and guards. He had dispatched Bunche[5] to America and hoped efforts there would bear fruit.

5 Assistant to Bernadotte and Acting Mediator after his death.

FRUS 1948, vol. 5, part 2, pp. 1295 – 6,
501. BB Palestine/8 – 748: Telegram

39 Recommendations of Count Bernadotte, United Nations Mediator in Palestine, 16 September 1948.

(b) The frontiers between the Arab and Jewish territories, in the absence of agreement between Arabs and Jews, should be established by the United Nations and delimited by a technical boundaries commission appointed by and responsible to the United Nations, with the following revisions in the boundaries broadly defined in the resolution of the General Assembly of 29 November in order to make them more equitable, workable and consistent with existing realities in Palestine.

I   The area known as the Negeb, south of a line running from the sea near Majdal east-southeast to Faluja (both of which places would be in Arab territory), should be defined as Arab territory;

II   The frontier should run from Faluja north-northeast to Ramleh and Lydda (both of which places would be in Arab territory), the frontier at Lydda then following the line established in the General Assembly resolution of 29 November;

III   Galilee should be defined as Jewish territory.

(c) The disposition of the territory of Palestine not included within the boundaries of the Jewish State should be left to the Governments of the Arab States in full consultation with the Arab inhabitants of Palestine, with the recommendation, however, that in view of the historical connexion and common interests of Transjordan and Palestine, there would be compelling reasons for merging the Arab territory of Palestine with the territory of Transjordan, subject to such frontier rectifications regarding other Arab States as may be found practicable and desirable.

(d) The United Nations, by declaration or other appropriate means, should undertake to provide special assurance that the boundaries between the Arab and Jewish territories shall be respected and maintained, subject only to such modifications as may be mutually agreed upon by the parties concerned.

(e) The port of Haifa, including the oil refineries and terminals, and without prejudice to their inclusion in the sovereign territory of the Jewish State or the administration of the city of Haifa, should be declared a free port, with assurances of free access for interested Arab countries and an undertaking on their part to place no obstacle in the way of oil deliveries by pipeline to the Haifa refineries, whose distribution would continue on the basis of the historical pattern.

(f) The airport of Lydda should be declared a free airport with assurances of access to it and employment of its facilities for Jerusalem and interested Arab countries.

(g) The City of Jerusalem, which should be understood as covering the area defined in the resolution of the General Assembly of 29 November, should be treated separately and should be placed under effective United Nations control with maximum feasible local autonomy for its Arab and Jewish communities, with full safeguards for the protection of the Holy Places and sites and free access to them, and for religious freedom.

(h) The right of unimpeded access to Jerusalem, by road, rail or air, should be fully respected by all parties.

(i) The right of the Arab refugees to return to their homes in Jewish-controlled territory at the earliest possible date should be affirmed by the United Nations, and their repatriation, resettlement and economic and social rehabilitation, and payment of adequate compensation for the property of those choosing not to return, should be supervised and assisted by the United Nations conciliation commission described in paragraph (k) below.

(j) The political, economic, social and religious rights of all Arabs in the Jewish territory of Palestine and of all Jews in the Arab territory of Palestine should be fully guaranteed and respected by the authorities. The conciliation commission provided for in the following paragraph should supervise the observation of this guarantee. It should also lend its good offices, on the invitation of the parties, to any efforts toward exchanges of populations with a view to eliminating troublesome minority problems, and on the basis of adequate compensation for property owned.

(k) In view of the special nature of the Palestine problem and the dangerous complexities of Arab-Jewish relationships, the United Nations should establish a Palestine conciliation commission. This commission, which should be appointed for a limited period, should be responsible to the United Nations and act under its authority.

> UNO GAOR, Third Session, Supplement No. 11 (A/648), 16 September 1948, *Progress Report of the United Nations Mediator in Palestine*, Part 1, VIII

40   The Egyptian-Israeli General Armistice Agreement, signed at Rhodes, 24 February 1949

Article I

With a view to promoting the return to permanent peace in Palestine and in recognition of the importance in this regard of mutual assurances concerning the future military operations of the Parties, the following principles, which shall be fully observed by both Parties during the Armistice, are hereby affirmed:

1   The injunction of the Security Council against resort to military force in the settlement of the Palestine question shall henceforth be scrupulously respected by both Parties.

2   No aggressive action by the armed forces — land, sea, or air — of either Party shall be undertaken, planned, or threatened against the people or the armed forces of the other; it being understood that the use of the term 'planned' in this context has no bearing on normal staff planning as generally practiced in military organizations.

3   The right of each Party to its security and freedom from fear of attack by the armed forces of the other shall be fully respected.

4   The establishment of an armistice between the armed forces of the two Parties is accepted as an indispensable step toward the liquidation of armed conflict and the restoration of peace in Palestine.

Article II

1   In pursuance of the foregoing principles and of the resolutions of the Security Council of 4 and 16 November 1948, a general armistice between the armed forces of the two Parties — land, sea and air — is hereby established.

2   No element of the land, sea or air military or para-military forces of either Party, including non-regular forces, shall commit any warlike or hostile act against the military or para-military forces of the other Party, or against civilians in territory under the control of that Party; or shall advance beyond or pass over for any purpose whatsoever the Armistice Demarcation Line set forth in Article VI of this Agreement except as provided in Article III of this Agreement; and elsewhere shall not violate the international frontier; or enter into or pass through the waters within three miles of the coastline of the other Party.

Article IV

With specific reference to the implementation of the resolutions of the Security Council of 4 and 16 November 1948, the following principles and purposes are affirmed:

1 The principle that no military or political advantage should be gained under the truce ordered by the Security Council is recognized.

2 It is also recognized that the basic purposes and spirit of the Armistice would not be served by the restoration of previously held military positions, changes from those now held other than as specifically provided for in this Agreement, or by the advance of the military forces of either side beyond positions held at the time this Armistice Agreement is signed.

3 It is further recognized that rights, claims or interests of a non-military character in the area of Palestine covered by this Agreement may be asserted by either Party, and that these, by mutual agreement being excluded from the Armistice negotiations, shall be, at the discretion of the Parties, the subject of later settlement. It is emphasized that it is not the purpose of this Agreement to establish, to recognize, to strengthen, or to weaken or nullify, in any way, any territorial, custodial or other rights, claims or interests which may be asserted by either Party in the area of Palestine or any part or locality thereof covered by this Agreement, whether such asserted rights, claims or interests derive from Security Council resolutions, including the resolution of 4 November 1948 and the Memorandum of 13 November 1948 for its implementation, or from any other source. The provisions of this Agreement are dictated exclusively by military considerations and are valid only for the period of the Armistice.

Article V

1 The line described in Article VI of this Agreement shall be designated as the Armistice Demarcation Line and is delineated in pursuance of the purpose and intent of the resolutions of the Security Council of 4 and 16 November 1948.

2 The Armistice Demarcation Line is not to be construed in any sense as a political or territorial boundary, and is delineated without prejudice to rights, claims and positions of either Party to the Armistice as regards ultimate settlement of the Palestine question.

.   .   .

Article XI

No provision of this Agreement shall in any way prejudice the rights, claims and positions of either Party hereto in the ultimate peaceful settlement of the Palestine question.

> UNO SCOR, Fourth Year, Special Supplement No. 3, Doc. S/1264/Rev. 1

41 Letter from the Chairman of the United Nations Conciliation Commission for Palestine to the Secretary-General analysing the position of the Palestinian refugees, 17 November 1949

THE PROBLEM

The Arab refugees – nearly three-quarters of a million men, women and children – are the symbol of the paramount political issue in the Near East. Their plight is the aftermath of an armed struggle between Arabs and Israelis, a struggle marked by a truce that was broken and an armistice from which a peace settlement has not emerged.

Before the hostilities in Palestine these families lived in that section of Palestine on the Israeli side of the present armistice lines. Abandoning their homes and villages, their fields and orange groves, their shops and benches, they fled to nearby Arab lands. Tens of thousands are in temporary camps; some are in caves; the majority have found shelter in Arab towns and villages, in mosques, churches, monasteries, schools and abandoned buildings. Some seventeen thousand Jewish refugees, too, fled from their homes in and around Jerusalem and territories on the Arab side of the armistice lines. They entered into Israel where most of them have now been absorbed.

The worsening plight of the refugees as an obstacle to peace in Palestine prompted the General Assembly of the United Nations in November 1948 to appeal to the nations of the world for funds to provide food, clothing and shelter for the refugees. This emergency relief programme was established with great despatch. Governments contributed in the hope that conciliation would produce peace and lay the basis for a permanent solution for the refugees.

On 11 December 1948 the General Assembly adopted a resolution stating: ' . . . that the refugees wishing to return to their homes and live at peace with their neighbours should be permitted to do so at the earliest possible date, and that compensation should be paid for the property of those choosing not to return . . . '

The same resolution established a Conciliation Commission for Palestine to negotiate a settlement of outstanding differences between Israel and the Arab States of Egypt, Iraq, Jordan, Lebanon, Saudi-Arabia, Syria and the Yemen.

No settlement has been reached.

The Arab refugees have not been able to return to their homes because Israel will not admit them. Israel has to date offered to repatriate only 100,000, and only as a part of a general peace settlement of all other issues.

The Arab refugees have not been able to gain a livlihood in the Arab lands where they are because there is insufficient opportunity for them to do so.

The Arab refugees have not yet received compensation for the property they abandoned, nor have the Jewish refugees in their turn.

The refugees are still on relief.

United Nations funds so far subscribed for the feeding of refugees will not last through the winter.

.   .   .

RECOMMENDATIONS

In the light of these findings, the Economic Survey Mission[1] makes the following recommendations, which are explained later in the report.

.   .   .

3   An agency should be established to organize and, on or after 1 April 1950, direct, the programmes of relief and public works herein recommended.[2]

.   .   .

DISCUSSION OF FINDINGS AND RECOMMENDATIONS

THE PALESTINE REFUGEES

Their number. No one knows exactly how many refugees there are. After considering all available information, the Economic Survey Mission estimated that the total number of refugees does not exceed 774,000, including 48,000 in Israel, of whom 17,000 are Jews. Of this 774,000 it is estimated that 147,000 are self-supporting or otherwise provided for. This leaves 627,000 refugees at present dependent upon

1   The UN Economic Survey Mission was deputed by the Conciliation Commission for Palestine to examine economic conditions in the Middle East.
2   This became the United Nations Relief and Works Agency for Palestine Refugees in the Near East (UNRWA).

United Nations relief. In addition, the Mission recommends the inclusion of 25,000 Arabs who, though living in their original homes in Arab territory, are destitute through being separated from their lands by the Armistice Agreements. This would bring the total figure of persons who are eligible for relief from the United Nations to 652,000. *Their location.* Where did the refugees go when they left their homes? About 70,000 crossed the Jordan River to the east and are now in the Hashemite Kingdom of Jordan. About 97,000 fled into Lebanon, just north of Galilee. Some 75,000 are clustered near the south and western boundaries of Syria, and in and around Damascus and other towns. About 280,000 are in that part of Palestine not occupied by Israel — west of the Jordan — from Jenin in the north to Jericho and the Arab portion of Jerusalem and on beyond to Bethlehem in the south. About 4,000 crossed the desert to Baghdad, far to the east. In addition, some 31,000 Arabs and 17,000 Jews, classed as refugees by the international relief agencies, are in Israel.

The influx of these destitute families into already crowded areas, notably Arab Palestine, the Gaza strip and the western part of the Kingdom of Jordan, has aggravated the already depressed standard of life in these regions. This may help to account for the 940,000 rations now issued daily, as against the 652,000 recommended in this report. *Their effect on local resources.* The effects of the influx of the refugees upon the resources of the Arab States can be suggested by comparing the number of refugees to the total population of the areas where they are chiefly located.

The population of the Gaza strip, before the Arab-Israeli hostilities, was about 70,000. Refugees have swelled the population to about 270,000 in an area of less than 150 square miles. Gaza is now cut off by the armistice lines from its normal trade area; most of the farmlands normally tilled by the villagers in the Gaza strip are now inaccessible to them, because the armistice line separates the farmer from his land. He can see his land across the line, but he enters upon it to tend his orange groves or harvest his crop at the peril of his life.

Arab Palestine, that portion of eastern Palestine not occupied by Israeli troops, had an estimated population of 460,000 before the outbreak of hostilities. To this has been added about 280,000 refugees, an increase of 60 per cent.

·   ·   ·

The refugees' dilemma. Why don't the refugees return to their homes and solve their own problem? That is what the great majority of them want to do. They believe as a matter of right and justice they should be permitted to return to their homes, their farms and villages, and the coastal cities of Haifa and Jaffa whence many of them came.

They are encouraged to believe this remedy open to them because the General Assembly of the United Nations said so in its resolution of 11 December 1948. For purely psychological resons, easily under-standable, the refugees set great store by the assurance contained in this resolution. Most men in their position, given a choice between working in a foreign land or returning to their homes and to conditions understood and experienced from youth, would strain towards their homes, even were they told that, in their absence, conditions had so changed that they would never be happy there again. They would be reluctant to believe it. They would suspect a trap to hold them in exile until it was too late for them to return. Even if they were told their houses had been destroyed, they would still claim that the land remained. This seems a final argument to farm people.

But, the repatriation of Arab refugees requires political decisions outside the competence of the Economic Survey Mission.

Why don't the refugees go somewhere else? Why not resettle them in less congested lands?

There are several reasons. The refugees do not take kindly to moving again — unless it be a return to their homes, a prospect they cling to because of the General Assembly's resolution. Moreover, the Arab Governments have made it clear to the Mission that they feel bound to respect the wishes of the refugees. Resettlement of the refugees outside of Palestine is a political issue poised against the issues of repatriation, compensation of the refugees and a final territorial settlement. Finally, less congested lands are not available for the settlement of additional population until much money has been spent and work done to make the land suitable for cultivation or for industrial development.

In these circumstances, the only immediate constructive step in sight is to give the refugees an opportunity to work where they now are.

> UNO GAOR, Fourth Session, *Ad Hoc* Political Committee, Annex to the summary records of meetings, vol. I, 1949, doc. A/1106, First Interim Report of the United Nations Economic Survey Mission for the Middle East.

V

The Egyptian Revolution and the Suez Crisis

The setbacks suffered by the Arab armies in the 1948 – 1949 war accelerated revolutionary aspirations which had long been maturing in a number of countries, notably in Egypt, whose military performance had been impaired by corruption in government. By October 1949, the Free Officers movement, under the presidency of Gamal Abdul Nasser and including Anwar al-Sadat and Abdul Hakim Amer, was working to convert the army into a revolutionary base. When they mounted their successful *coup* against the monarchy on 23 July 1953, their titular leader was General Muhammad Naguib. The announcement of the revolution, issued by the Free Officers in Naguib's name, drew attention to the corruption and instability of the preceding years (42). Naguib and Nasser vied for power in republican Egypt, the issue being resolved in the latter's favour in a power struggle in March-April 1954. Although Naguib remained as president until the following November, Nasser was increasingly in effective control of the country.

Middle East tension increased sharply in 1955. Using as his justification Palestinian raids from Egyptian-occupied territory, the Israeli defence minister, David Ben-Gurion, ordered a major raid into the Gaza strip on 28 February 1955. His principal object was to demonstrate Israeli military strength to the new Egyptian regime and to the western powers which were then negotiating for Arab support in the Cold War. Probably he also wished to reassure an Israeli public opinion which had been rattled by the failure of intelligence operations in Egypt and the continuing denial of the Suez Canal to their shipping. The Security Council resolution condemning the raid, submitted by the United States, Britain and France, indicates Israel's diplomatic isolation (43). In an attempt to build up Egypt's military potential, in September 1955 Nasser concluded an arms agreement with the Soviet Union, officially disguised as being with Czechoslovakia. In document 44 he gives his reasons for this dramatic step, which gave the Soviet Union a significant voice in Middle Eastern affairs for the first time.

Faced with apparently intractable problems of poverty and expanding population, Nasser concentrated his hopes for economic improvement on the proposed construction of the Aswan High Dam, which, it was anticipated, would generate cheap hydro-electric power and expand the area of land available for cultivation. He conducted negotiations with the United States and Britain for the necessary financial assistance to be provided through the World Bank, but on 19 July 1956, the Americans, annoyed by his apparent alignment with the Soviet Union and concerned at the possible effect of his arms purchases on Egypt's ability to sustain her contribution to the building of the dam, withdrew their offer of help; the British, sensitive to accusations of favouring him at the expense of their Arab allies, followed suit. The American announcement (45) was left bland in the hope of muting Nasser's reaction, but on 26 July he retaliated with the nationalization of the Suez Canal Company (46).

In early August, the British government, having conjured up Nasser as the new Hitler and viewing his action as a threat to their lines of communication, combined with the French, who believed him to be behind their costly Algerian war, in preparing a military expedition to restore the canal's international status and perhaps initiate a change of regime in Cairo. On 29 October, Israel mounted an invasion of Sinai designed to remove guerrilla bases, weaken the Egyptian army and free the Gulf of Aqaba for her shipping (47). The following day, Britain and France addressed ultimata to Israel and Egypt, threatening intervention on the canal if their terms were ignored (48). In rejecting their demands, Nasser speculated that the crisis had been engineered through an Anglo-French-Israeli conspiracy (49), a charge the British repudiated. Later revelations, however, confirmed that the idea of inviting an Israeli attack in order to provide the pretext for Anglo-French intervention had been suggested to the British prime minister, Anthony Eden, by French emissaries on 14 October and that details of the scheme had been formalized at talks attended by representatives of the three governments at Sèvres between 22 and 24 October. On 5 November, Anglo-French airborne units landed at Port Said and Port Fuad, to be followed the next day by amphibious troops. By then, however, the cessation of hostilities between Israel and Egypt and the United Nations resolution of 4 November (50) had removed the ostensible reason for intervention. Faced with worldwide hostility and American financial pressure applied through the International Monetary Fund, the British government felt they had no alternative but to abandon the operation forthwith.

The final four documents in this chapter illustrate the diplomatic compromises whereby Israel was induced to withdraw her troops from Sinai. Although the fighting had left her militarily strong there, her continued presence was unacceptable to the United States which exerted strong pressure for her evacuation. During a series of exchanges in January-February 1957 involving the Israelis with the Americans and the United Nations Secretary-General, Dag Hammarskjöld, this was conceded in return for the stationing of the United Nations Emergency Force (UNEF) along the 1949 armistice demarcation line. Document 51 underlines Israel's continuing diplomatic weakness, while document 52 sets out UNEF's terms of reference. The nature of Hammarskjöld's guarantees on the Gulf of Aqaba and Gaza, felt by Israel to be basic to her security, are given in document 53. In document 54, the Israeli Foreign Minister, Golda Meir, trenchantly defined these agreements in a speech basic to an understanding of the 1967 crisis. What had been agreed defined the nature of Israeli-Egyptian relations for the next decade, with Israeli shipping passing through the Straits of Tiran and the ending of guerrilla operations from Gaza.

42 Proclamation issued by the Egyptian Free Officers in the name of General Muhammad Naguib, 23 July 1952

Egypt has undergone a critical time in its recent history. It has been a period of graft, corruption and government instability. All these factors had a great influence on the Army. Biased persons and those who received bribes contributed to our defeat in the Palestine war. But the post-war period was controlled by elements of corruption, and traitors plotted against the Army which was ruled either by an ignorant traitor or by an intriguer so that Egypt might become a country without a defending army. Consequently, we have purged ourselves. Our affairs inside the Army have been placed in the hands of men in whose ability, character and patriotism we have faith. No doubt the whole of Egypt will welcome this news.

As regards those we have arrested, namely, former military personnel, no harm shall be done to them. They will be released at the appropriate time. I assure the Egyptian people that the entire Army is now working in the interests of the country, within the Constitution and without any designs. I take this opportunity to ask the people not to permit any traitor to resort to acts of sabotage or violence, as these are not in the interests of Egypt. Any such action will be met with unparalleled firmness and the offender will immediately be punished for treason. The Army will undertake this responsibility in cooperation with the police. I want to assure our brother foreigners of the safety of their business, lives and properties. The Army considers itself completely responsible for them. God is the giver of success.

SWB, Part IV, no. 280, 29 July 1952.

43　Security Council resolution on the Gaza raid, 29 March 1955

The Security Council,

Having heard the report of the Chief of Staff of the United Nations Truce Supervision Organization and statements by the representatives of Egypt and Israel,

Noting that the Egyptian-Israeli Mixed Armistice Commission on 6 March 1955 determined that a 'prearranged and planned attack ordered by Israel authorities' was 'committed by Israel regular army forces against the Egyptian regular army force' in the Gaza strip on 28 February 1955.

1　Condemns this attack as a violation of the cease-fire provisions of the Security Council resolution of 15 July 1948 and as inconsistent with the obligations of the parties under the General Armistice Agreement between Egypt and Israel and under the United Nations Charter;

2　Calls again upon Israel to take all necessary measures to prevent such actions;

3　Expresses its conviction that the maintenance of the General Armistice Agreement is threatened by any deliberate violation of that agreement by one of the parties to it, and that no progress towards the return of permanent peace in Palestine can be made unless the parties comply strictly with their obligations under the General Armistice Agreement and the cease-fire provisions of the resolution of 15 July 1948.

UNO SCOR, *Supplement for January, February and March 1955*, doc. S/3378

44   Statement by Colonel Nasser on Egypt's arms agreement with Czechoslovakia, 30 September 1955

Ever since the first day of the revolution we have persistently asked for arms. Because of the disturbances in Egypt, Britain desisted from fulfilling the agreement we concluded with her prior to 1952. We also asked France and the USA; but we met with many difficulties, although a senior official of the US State Department in October 1952 promised to supply us with arms. We prepared a list of our requirements and sent a delegation to Washington, but the delegation returned empty-handed after long talks. This was because of British pressure at the time. France did not want to supply us with arms. Belgium — under British pressure, no doubt — acted likewise. At that time Sweden also refused.

Britain promised to meet our needs in arms as soon as we signed an agreement with her concerning the Suez Canal base. We therefore approached Britain again after the agreement was signed; and we received from her equipment which Egypt had contracted to buy before the revolution and of which she had already paid 80 per cent of the cost. From the USA we received only words and promises; while she did not refuse to supply us with arms, we never received any arms from her.

However, we concluded an agreement with France. I told the French Ambassador in Cairo that, as long as his country supplied Israel with arms, she should supply us as well. Agreement was reached, but France cancelled this two weeks ago; she wanted us to give a pledge to overlook her policy in North Africa, in return for her arms.

I also asked for arms from the USSR and Czechoslovakia. I told the British and US Ambassadors last June, that if their countries did not supply me with arms, I would have to obtain them from the USSR. I stated that it was not possible for me to remain silent while Israel imported weapons for her army from several sources and imposed a constant threat on us.

.   .   .

While France cancels her agreement with us, she is fulfilling an agreement with Israel, as stated in the official French gazette. Israeli newspapers, too, have reported that Israel has received 100 tanks, Mystere jet aircraft and 155mm guns from France.

I felt a daily growing Israeli threat to Egypt. This feeling grew when

I read the statements of Ben-Gurion and other Israeli leaders urging the need for expansion and for domination of the Arabs. I naturally accepted the arms deal which was offered by Czechoslovakia on a purely commercial basis. We therefore did not find any need to conclude a contract with the USSR, since the entire question was no more than the need to obtain arms from any source at any price.

SWB, Part IV, no. 609, 4 Oct. 1955

45 American statement on the withdrawal of their offer of financial aid to Egypt for the building of the Aswan High Dam, 19 July 1956

At the request of the Government of Egypt, the United States joined in December 1955 with the United Kingdom and with the World Bank in an offer to assist Egypt in the construction of a high dam on the Nile at Aswan. This project is one of great magnitude. It would require an estimated 12 to 16 years to complete at a total cost estimated at some $1,300,000,000, of which over $900,000,000 represents local currency requirements. It involves not merely the rights and interests of Egypt but of others whose waters are contributory, including Sudan, Ethiopia, and Uganda.

The December offer contemplated an extension by the United States and United Kingdom of grant aid to help finance certain early phases of the work, the effects of which would be confined solely to Egypt, with the understanding that accomplishment of the project as a whole would require a satisfactory solution of the question of Nile water rights. Another important consideration bearing upon the feasibility of the undertaking, and thus the practicability of American aid, was Egyptian readiness and ability to concentrate its economic resources upon this vast construction program.

Developments within the succeeding seven months have not been favourable to the success of the project, and the US Government has concluded that it is not feasible in present circumstances to participate in the project. Agreement by the riparian states has not been achieved, and the ability of Egypt to devote adequate resources to assure the project's success has become more uncertain than at the time the offer was made.

This decision in no way reflects or involves any alteration in the friendly relations of the Government and people of the United States toward the Government and people of Egypt.

The United States remains deeply interested in the welfare of the Egyptian people and in the development of the Nile. It is prepared to consider at an appropriate time and at the request of the riparian states what steps might be taken toward a more effective utilization of the water resources of the Nile for the benefit of the peoples of the region. Furthermore, the United States remains ready to assist Egypt in its effort to improve the economic condition of its people and is prepared, through its appropriate agencies, to discuss these matters within the context of funds appropriated by the Congress.

DSB, 30 July 1956

46   Speech by President Nasser justifying nationalization of the Suez Canal Company, 28 July 1956

The uproar which we anticipated has been taking place in London and Paris. This tremendous uproar is not supported by reason or logic. It is backed only by imperialist methods, by the habits of blood-sucking and of usurping rights, and by interference in the affairs of other countries. An unjustified uproar arose in London, and yesterday Britain submitted a protest to Egypt. I wonder what was the basis of this protest by Britain to Egypt? The Suez Canal Company is an Egyptian company, subject to Egyptian sovereignty. When we nationalized the Suez Canal Company, we only nationalized an Egyptian limited company, and by doing so we exercised a right which stems from the very core of Egyptian sovereignty. What right has Britain to interfere in our internal affairs? What right has Britain to interfere in our affairs and our questions? When we nationalized the Suez Canal Company, we only performed an act stemming from the very heart of our sovereignty. The Suez Canal Company is a limited company, awarded a concession by the Egyptian Government in 1865 to carry out its tasks. Today we withdraw the concession in order to do the job ourselves.

Although we have withdrawn this concession, we shall compensate shareholders of the company, despite the fact that they usurped our rights. Britain usurped 44 per cent of the shares free of charge. Today we shall pay her for her 44 per cent of the shares. We do not treat her as she treated us. We are not usurping the 44 per cent as she did. We do not tell Britain that we shall usurp her right as she usurped ours, but we tell her that we shall compensate her and forget the past.

The Suez Canal would have been restored to us in 12 years. What would have happened in 12 years' time? Would an uproar have been raised? What has happened now has disclosed hidden intentions and has unmasked Britain. If the canal was to fall to us in 12 years, why should it not be restored to us now? Why should it cause an uproar? We understand by this that they had no intention of fulfilling this pledge 12 years from now. What difference is it if the canal is restored to us now or in 12 years' time? Why should Britain say this will affect shipping in the canal? Would it have affected shipping 12 years hence?

.   .   .

Shipping in the Suez Canal has been normal for the past 48 hours from the time of nationalization until now. Shipping continued and is normal. We nationalized the company. We have not interfered with shipping, and we are facilitating shipping matters. However, I emphatically warn the imperialist countries that their tricks, provocations and interference will be the reason for any hindrance to shipping. I place full responsibility on Britain and France for any curtailment of shipping in the Suez Canal when I state that Egypt will maintain freedom of shipping in the Suez Canal, and that since Egypt nationalized the Suez Canal Company shipping has been normal. Even before that we maintained freedom of shipping in the canal. Who has protected the canal? The canal has been under Egyptian protection because it is part of Egypt and we are the ones who should ensure freedom of shipping. We protect it today, we protected it a month ago, and we protected it for years because it is our territory and a part of our territory. Today we shall continue to protect the canal. But, because of the tricks they are playing, I hold Britain and France responsible for any consequences which may affect shipping.

.   .   .

Compatriots, we shall maintain our independence and sovereignty. The Suez Canal Company has become our property, and the Egyptian flag flies over it. We shall hold it with our blood and strength, and we shall meet aggression with aggression and evil with evil. We shall proceed towards achieving dignity and prestige for Egypt and building a sound national economy and true freedom. Peace be with you.

SWB, Part IV, Daily Series, no. 6, 30 July 1956

47   Speech to the Security Council by Abba Eban, Israel, on his country's offensive in Sinai, 30 October 1956

33   At this morning's meeting I defined the objective of the security measures which the Israel defence forces have felt bound to take in the Sinai Peninsula in the exercise of our country's inherent right of self-defence. The object of the operations is to eliminate the Egyptian *fedayeen*[1] bases from which armed Egyptian units, under the special care and authority of Mr Nasser, invade Israel territory for purposes of murder, sabotage and the creation of permanent insecurity to peaceful life.

34   World opinion is naturally asking itself what these *fedayeen* units are, what their activities imply for Israel's security, whether their actions in the past and their plans for the future are really full of peril for Israel, and whether this peril is so acute that Israel may reasonably regard elimination of the danger as a primary condition of its security and indeed of its existence.

35   The Government of Israel is the representative of a people endowed with a mature understanding of international facts. We are not unaware of the limitations of our strength. We fully understand how certain measures might at first sight evoke a lack of comprehension even in friendly minds. Being a democracy, we work under the natural restraints of a public opinion which compels us to weigh drastic choices with care and without undue precipitation. It is therefore a Government which governs its actions by its single exclusive aim of securing life, security and opportunities of self-development for the people whom it represents, whilst also safeguarding the honour and trust of millions linked to it by the strongest ties of fraternity.

36   In recent months and days the Government of Israel has had to face a tormenting question: Do its obligations under the United Nations Charter require us to resign ourselves to the existence of uninterrupted activity to the south and north and east of our country, of armed bands practising open warfare against us and working from their bases in the Sinai Peninsula and elsewhere for the maintenance of carefully regulated invasions of our homes, or lands and our very lives, or, on the other hand, are we acting in accordance with an inherent right of self-defence when having found no other remedy for over two years, we cross the frontier against those who have no scruple or hesitation in crossing the frontier against us?

1   Palestinian Arab guerrillas, lit. 'those ready to sacrifice themselves'.

UNO SCOR, Eleventh Year, 749th Meeting

48 The Anglo-French ultimatum to Egypt, 30 October 1956

The Governments of the United Kingdom and France have taken note of the outbreak of hostilities between Israel and Egypt. This event threatens to disrupt the freedom of navigation through the Suez Canal, on which the economic life of many nations depends. The Governments of the United Kingdom and France are resolved to do all in their power to bring about the early cessation of hostilities and to safeguard the free passage of the Canal. They accordingly request the Government of Egypt:

(a) to stop all warlike action on land, sea and air forthwith;

(b) to withdraw all Egyptian military forces to a distance of ten miles from the Canal; and

(c) in order to guarantee freedom of transit through the Canal by the ships of all nations and in order to separate the belligerents, to accept the temporary occupation by Anglo-French forces of key positions at Port Said, Ismailia and Suez.

The United Kingdom and French Governments request an answer to this communication within twelve hours. If at the expiration of that time one or both Governments have not undertaken to comply with the above requirements, United Kingdom and French forces will intervene in whatever strength may be necessary to secure compliance.

A similar communication has been sent to the Government of Israel.

UNO SCOR, Elventh Year, 749th Meeting

49 President Nasser's response to the Anglo-French ultimatum, 1 November 1956

Today, we face these plots as one, one heart, one man. These plots began with the conspiracy of Britain, France and Israel. Israel suddenly on Monday 29 October began an offensive, for no other reason except Britain's rancour. Our armed forces rose and did their duty with rare gallantry. Our air force did its duty with eternal courage, in the history of the homeland. When Israel attacked,

Britain announced that she would not seize the opportunity. But when it appeared that Egypt was able to dominate the battle, an Anglo-French ultimatum was presented.

This ultimatum asked for a halt to the fighting—while the Israeli forces were inside Egyptian territory—the aggressor Israeli forces. It asked Egypt and Israel to withdraw 10km (sic) from the Suez Canal. It then asked Egypt and also Israel to agree to the occupation of Port Said, Ismailia and Suez by the Anglo-French forces, for the protection of shipping in the Canal. This happened at a time when navigation was in progress and was not threatened. This happened while the Egyptian forces were concentrating to face the aggressor Israeli forces, and the Egyptian forces were repelling the Israeli forces.

In her ultimatum Britain said that if a reply was not received within 12 hours she would act to execute the ultimatum. Do we agree to the occupation by Britain and France of part of Egyptian territory? Do we willingly agree to such occupation? Or do we fight for the freedom of our homeland, for the safety of our territory, for honour and for dignity? After this ultimatum Egypt decided upon her attitude. It was this: It is impossible for her to permit, it is impossible for her to accept, and it is impossible for her to agree to the occupation of Port Said, Ismailia and Suez by foreign forces—Anglo-French—and declared that this was a violation of her freedom—the freedom, sovereignty and dignity of the Egyptian people.

> SWB, Part IV, Daily Series, no. 88, 3
> Nov. 1956

50   General Assembly resolution, 4 November 1956

The General Assembly,
Bearing in mind the urgent necessity of facilitating compliance with its resolution 997(ES-I) of 2 November 1956,[1]
Requests, as a matter of priority, the Secretary-General to submit to it within forty-eight hours a plan for the setting up, with the consent of the nations concerned, of an emergency international United Nations Force to secure and supervise the cessation of hostilities in accordance with all the terms of the aforementioned resolution.

> UNO GAOR, First Emergency Special
> Session, Supplement No. 1, resolution
> 998(ES-I)

---

1   This called for a cease-fire and a halt to military movements into the area.

51 General Assembly resolution, 2 February 1957

The General Assembly,

.   .   .

1 *Deplores* the non-compliance of Israel to complete its withdrawal behind the armistice demarcation line despite the repeated requests of the General Assembly;
2 *Calls upon* Israel to complete its withdrawal behind the armistice demarcation line without further delay.

> UNO GAOR, Eleventh Session, Supplement No. 17, resolution 1124 (XI)

52 General Assembly resolution, 2 February 1957

The General Assembly,
Having received the report of the Secretary-General of 24 January 1957,
Recognizing that withdrawal by Israel must be followed by action which would assure progress towards the creation of peaceful conditions,
1 *Notes with appreciation* the Secretary-General's report and the measures therein to be carried out upon Israel's complete withdrawal;
2 *Calls upon* the Governments of Egypt and Israel scrupulously to observe the provisions of the General Armistice Agreement between Egypt and Israel of 24 February 1949;
3 *Considers* that, after full withdrawal of Israel from the Sharm el Sheikh and Gaza areas, the scrupulous maintenance of the Armistice Agreement requires the placing of the United Nations Emergency Force on the Egyptian-Israel armistice demarcation line and the implementation of other measures as proposed in the Secretary-General's report, with due regard to the considerations set out therein with a view to assist in achieving situations conducive to the maintenance of peaceful conditions in the area;
4 *Requests* the Secretary-General, in consultation with the parties concerned, to take steps to carry out these measures and to report, as appropriate, to the General Assembly.

> UNO GAOR, Eleventh Session, Supplement No. 17, resolution 1125(XI)

53   Secretary-General Dag Hammarskjöld's memorandum on his
     discussion with Abba Eban on 25 February 1957 over UNEF's
     role in the Gulf of Aqaba and Straits of Tiran

A   The representative of Israel, stating that his Government's
primary concern in this area was in measures designed to reduce the
risk of reoccurence of acts of belligerency after the withdrawal of
Israel, raised the following three questions:
1   Following the withdrawal of Israel's forces, would the function of
the Emergency Force be as described in the Secretary-General's
memorandum of 5 January in response to Mr Eban's questions,
namely, the prevention of possible acts of belligerency?
2   In connexion with the duration of UNEF's deployment in the
Sharm-el-Sheikh area, would the Secretary-General give notice to the
General Assembly of the United Nations before UNEF would be
withdrawn from the area, with or without Egyptian insistence, or
before the Secretary-General would agree to its withdrawal?
3   The question of adding a naval unit to UNEF for purposes of
instituting a United Nations naval patrol in the Gulf of Aqaba and
Straits of Tiran to ensure free and innocent passage.
B   The responses of the Secretary-General to these questions are
summarized as follows:
1   With regard to the function of UNEF in the prevention of
belligerency, the answer is affirmative, subject to the qualification
that UNEF is never to be used in such a way as to force a solution of any
controversial political or legal problem.
2   On the question of notification to the General Assembly, the
Secretary-General wanted to state his view at a later meeting. An
indicated procedure would be for the Secretary-General to inform the
Advisory Committee on the United Nations Emergency Force, which
would determine whether the matter should be brought to the
attention of the Assembly.
3   The question of the naval unit, in that it implies a function which
would go beyond the prevention of belligerent acts as envisaged in the
basic General Assembly resolutions, would be beyond the competence
of the Secretary-General on the basis of those resolutions.

                              UNO   GAOR,   Eleventh   Session,
                         Annexes, doc. A/3563

54 Speech by Golda Meir, Israeli Foreign Minister, to the General Assembly, 1 March 1957

The Government of Israel is now in a position to announce its plans for full and prompt withdrawal from the Sharm-el-Sheikh area and the Gaza strip, in compliance with General Assembly resolution 1124(XI) of 2 February 1957.

2 We have repeatedly stated that Israel has no interest in the strip of land overlooking the western coast of the Gulf of Aqaba. Our sole purpose has been to ensure that, on the withdrawal of Israeli forces, continued freedom of navigation will exist for Israel and international shipping in the Gulf of Aqaba and the Straits of Tiran. Such freedom of navigation is a vital national interest for Israel, but it is also of importance and legitimate concern to the maritime Powers and to many States whose economies depend upon trade and navigation between the Red Sea and the Mediterranean.

.   .   .

11 The Government of Israel believes that the Gulf of Aqaba comprehends international waters and that no nation has the right to prevent free and innocent passage in the Gulf and through the Straits giving access thereto, in accordance with the generally accepted definition of those terms in the law of the sea.

12 In its capacity as a littoral State, Israel will gladly offer port facilities to the ships of all nations and all flags exercising free passage in the Gulf of Aqaba. We have received with gratification the assurances of the leading maritime Powers that they foresee a normal and regular flow of traffic of all cargoes in the Gulf of Aqaba. Israel will do nothing to impede free and innocent passage by ships of Arab countries bound to Arab ports or to any other destination. Israel is resolved on behalf of vessels of Israel registry to exercise the right to free and innocent passage and is prepared to join with others to secure universal respect of this right. Israel will protect ships of its own flag exercising the right of free and innocent passage on the high seas and in international waters.

13 Interference, by armed force, with ships of Israel flag exercising free and innocent passage in the Gulf of Aqaba and through the Straits of Tiran, will be regarded by Israel as an attack entitling it to exercise its inherent right of self-defence under Article 51 of the United

Nations Charter and to take all such measures as are necessary to ensure the free and innocent passages of its ships in the Gulf and in the Straits.

UNO GAOR, Eleventh Session, 666th Plenary Meeting

VI

The Re-Birth of Palestinian Awareness and the June War of 1967

Despite President Nasser's immense popularity between 1956 and 1961, many Palestinians felt angry and frustrated that their cause had figured so little in the Suez affair and its aftermath. By 1959, a small group of exiles, prominent amongst whom was Yasser Arafat, had come together in a movement which came to be known as Fatah, the reverse acronym for *Harakat al-Tahrir al-Filastin*, or 'Movement for the Liberation of Palestine'. In the early 1960s, Nasser had to face mounting criticism, notably from Syria and Iraq, for his evident unwillingness to contemplate any confrontation with Israel. Arab frustrations came to be focused on Israel's intention to divert waters from the Jordan river to expand her area of cultivation. The Cairo summit conference, which Nasser convened to discuss the issue, while undertaking no overt actions against Israel, marked the revival of active recognition of Palestinian aspirations (55). Its sequel was the formation of the Palestine Liberation Organization (PLO). Fatah's expansion at this time owed much to the patronage of successive Syrian governments which saw in its activism a means of embarrassing Nasser and the PLO which he supported. Its first guerrilla operation in Israel on 1 January 1965, while militarily insignificant, inaugurated a new era in Middle Eastern affairs (56).

The immediate origins of the 1967 war can be found in the steady rise in tension between Israel and a new Syrian government which had come to power in February the previous year and gave increased backing to Fatah's guerrillas. Israeli resentment over this, as well as at Syrian harrassment of her northern settlements from artillery emplacements in the Golan heights, reached a peak on 7 April 1967 when a major air battle was fought between the two countries. On 13 May, believing an attack on Damascus to be imminent, Syria and the Soviet Union informed Nasser of large Israeli troop concentrations opposite the Golan heights (57, 58 and 63). Although this information was never substantiated, Nasser responded by reinforcing his troops in

Sinai and demanding the withdrawal of UNEF, which was agreed to by United Nations Secretary-General U Thant (58). In document 58 he also revealed that as a result of UNEF's neutralization he had ordered the blockade of the Straits of Tiran, an action which Israel had repeatedly emphasized she would regard as an act of aggression (54 and 59). Egypt's defence of the blockade is given in document 60. As emotions heightened throughout the Arab world and Israeli diplomatic efforts in Paris, London and Washington to break the blockade proved barren, Nasser's confidence increased. On 29 May, he proclaimed Egypt ready for the confrontation with Israel, expanding his aims to include a settlement of Palestinian rights (61). Israel's riposte came on 5 June with a devastating pre-emptive strike against neighbouring Arab air forces. In the following six days she inflicted decisive defeats on the Egyptian, Jordanian and Syrian armies, giving her control of the Sinai desert, east Jerusalem, the west bank of the Jordan, and the Golan heights. Her reasons for going to war are given by Foreign Minister Abba Eban in document 62. The war was an undisguised disaster for the Arabs. As the hostilities ended, Nasser broadcast reiterating his account of the origins of the crisis and announcing his resignation, something which a stunned Egyptian public refused to contemplate (63).

55   The Cairo Arab Summit Conference, January 1964

The Council of the Kings and Presidents of the Arab League States, in its first session held at the League headquarters in Cairo, from 13 till 16 January 1964, in accordance with the proposal of President Jamal Abd an-Nasir, the President of the UAR,[1] considering the threats and the continuous acts of aggression made by Israel since it evicted the Arab Palestinian people from their homeland and established an imperialist occupation force on their territory, and the fact that Israel exercises racial discrimination against the Arab minority, uses the policy of aggression and of accomplished fact as a basis, persists in ignoring the resolutions passed by the UN affirming this people's natural right to return to their homeland, disregards the frequent condemnations passed by the various organizations of the international organization—having discussed what Israel is about to do, (commit) a new and serious aggression against Arab waters by

1   United Arab Republic.

diverting the Jordan and (causing) grave damage to the rights of the Arabs who derive benefit from these waters, aiming thereby at realizing expansionist Zionist ambitions by bringing in more forces of aggression and establishing other centres threatening the security of the Arab countries as well as their progress and world peace — in order to carry out the justified duty of defence and in the belief of the sacred rights of the Arab Palestinian people to exercise self-determination and to liberate themselves from the Zionist imperialism in their country, and in the belief that Arab solidarity is the way to resist imperialist ambitions and to realize the just Arab common interests to raise the standard of living of the majority and to carry out the programmes of reconstruction and development, the Council has taken the necessary practical measures to resist the existing Zionist danger, whether it be in the field of defence, of technology or in that of organizing the Palestinian people to enable them to carry out their role in liberating their homeland and determining their destiny.

SWB ME/1456/A/1

56 Political statement of the Fatah forces, issued on the occasion of their first raid in Israel, 1 January 1965

Sixteen years have elapsed while our people live detached from their cause which has been shelved by the United Nations as a problem of displaced refugees, whereas the enemy plans with all his means, on the local and international levels, for an extended stay in our homeland, ignoring the heroic Palestinians.

In the light of this distressing fact, and because of the adverse effect of the lapse of time, the Assifa[1] forces [of Fatah] have been launched to reiterate to the enemy and the world in general that this people [of Palestine] did not die, and that armed revolution is the road to return and victory.

The Assifa forces, emanating from the will of the revolting masses, fully realize the scope of the battle both politically and militarily. But they seek to overcome all obstacles, relying on their own strength and on the potential of our Arab people.

This is our path and this is our march. The situation is serious. Martyrs have fallen and blood has been shed. Let us rise to the level of responsibility — the responsibility of an honourable battle — because

1 Fatah's name for its guerrilla forces, lit. 'Lightning'.

this first operation is nothing but the beginning of a war of liberation with a carefully planned and studied programme. In this historic and critical stage, we are eager to declare unequivocally that our military and political plans do not contradict the official Palestinian and Arab plans for the battle. The struggle for Palestine flows into one stream which begins and ends with the uprooting of the Zionist danger from our homeland. We thus appeal to the Arab nation and its leaders to rise up with their responsibilities to the national committed level. Our battle with Israel is a fierce one and warrants preparation and mobilization.

As far as we are concerned, we have started from a Palestinian position connected to the soils of the nation. The strongest force which directs us is our faith in this as the surest way to extricate our cause from the vicious circle in which it has been trapped. We depend on our Arab nation and its common struggle as well as on world forces of liberation. Regardless of sacrifice, our march will not come to a halt before the flag of Palestine is brandished once again in our dear homeland. We also vow to our people to continue on this path and not to relinquish our arms until victory is achieved.

The Assifa forces seize this opportunity to thank the Arab mass media and all the free and honest writers who have understood our position and supported, with great devotion, the blessed initiation of our struggle. We also appreciate the attitude of the Palestinian and Arab institutions and organizations which supported us and stood by our side. The Arab people are called upon to support the launching of our struggle and to increase their material and moral support until we achieve our goals of return and freedom.

PLO Information Bulletin, *Palestine,*
vol. 2, no.8

57   Syrian Foreign Ministry Statement, 13 May 1967

The Foreign Ministry has summoned the representatives accredited to the Syrian Arab Republic from States which are members of the UN Security Council and explained to them the plot which is being concocted by imperialist and Zionist quarters against Syria. Referring to the successive provocative statements made by officials in the occupied land, the Foreign Ministry explained to these representatives the prearranged aggressive role which Israel is preparing to carry out within the framework of this plot and stressed the following points:

1   The successive Israeli threats made by Eshkol, Abba Eban, Israel's Ambassador in Washington, its delegates at the Security Council and Israeli military personnel are merely new moves to prepare world opinion and to camouflage the forthcoming Zionist aggression and a provocative action against the Syrian Arab Republic.

.   .   .

3   The excuses given by Israel regarding the activities of the Palestinian fida'iyin and its holding the Syrian Arab Republic responsible for them is rejected internationally. This is because the Palestinian Arab people—more than half of whom still dwell on the West Bank outside the Zionist occupation, in Gaza, and in other Arab areas, and about 1,000,000 of whom still live in tents; this Arab people who are being exposed to annihilation, suffering the harshest conditions, and who have been awaiting justice at the hands of the United Nations since 1948—do not accept the guardianship of Syria, the UAR or any other country. In their legitimate struggle to liberate their usurped homeland, they do not seek the permission of anyone. This right is guaranteed by the UN principles and all earthly laws. Consequently, no Arab country can be held responsible for the struggle of the Palestinian Arab people. Israel's excuse in this respect is false and does not hold water on any international level.

4   Using the Palestinian Arab people's struggle as a pretext for launching aggression against Syria cannot hide the imperialist-Zionist-reactionary plot against our country. The details of this plot have been revealed to the Arab people and the whole world. It hinges on a large Israeli attack on various feeble pretexts to be followed by an attack by mercenaries and agents of Jordanian Intelligence with imperialist weapons which are currently being massed along Syria's borders. This is to be accompanied by the efforts of reaction and the remnants of agents who were affected by the revolution. All this is to take place under the protection and direction of world imperialism. This plot, which began with the abortive attack of 7 April, is being implemented again today in an open and exposed manner, because the revolution with its organized working masses, its pioneering party, and its interaction with all Arab progressive forces and the freedom forces of the world constitutes a real danger to the interests of imperialism, Zionism and reaction in the area. Consequently it now faces an open plot in which Israel serves as the head spear. This criminal Zionist role can never be hidden from the Arab people and world public opinion. It is a recurrence of what took place during the Suez invasion.

5   The revolutionary regime in Syria is the target of the Israeli aggression which imperialist and Zionist quarters are preparing. This is clear from the statements of the Zionist Army Chief of Staff Rabin. This aim became clear today in statements from Israeli sources which defined the aim of the aggression as the liquidation of the revolutionary regime in Syria. Anything to the contrary is a feeble excuse to deceive world public opinion. Such excuses will never deceive anyone and will not hide the truth about the imperialist role Israel is playing in the area against the interests of the Arab people.

.   .   .

8   While drawing the attention of diplomatic representatives and world public opinion to the Zionist plot that is being hatched against the Syrian Arab Republic, the Foreign Ministry places on Israel and its protectors the responsibility for what may occur in the area. It affirms the readiness of the Government and people to confront any aggression with all its resources, will, and determination which knows no hesitation or surrender. The aggression being prepared by the Zionist circles will not be confronted by Syria alone, but by all the progressive Arab countries. The joint defence agreements will be put into effect.[1] The aggression will also be confronted with the people's liberation war which will be waged by all the Arab masses.

SWB, ME/2466/A/7 – 9

58   President Nasser's speech at the Egyptian Advanced Air Headquarters, 22 May 1967

On 13 May we received accurate information that Israel was concentrating on the Syrian border huge armed forces of about 11 to 13 brigades. These forces were divided into two fronts, one south of Lake Tiberias and the other north of the lake. The decision made by Israel at this time was to carry out an attack against Syria starting on 17 May. On 14 May we took action, discussed the matter and contacted our Syrian brothers. The Syrians also had this information. Based on the information Lt-Gen, Mahmud Fawzi left for Syria to coordinate matters. We told them that we had decided that if Syria was attacked Egypt would enter the battle right from the start. This was the situation on 14 May; forces began to move in the direction of Sinai to take up their normal positions.

1   A defence agreement was signed between Egypt and Syria on 4 November 1966.

News agencies reported yesterday that these military movements must have been the result of a previously well laid plan. I say that the sequence of events determined the plan. We had no plan prior to 13 May because we believed that Israel would not have dared to make such an impertinent statement.

On 16 May we requested the withdrawal of the United Nations Emergency Force (UNEF) in a letter from Lt-Gen. Mahmud Fawzi. We requested the complete withdrawal of the UNEF. A major world-wide campaign, led by the United States, Britain and Canada, began opposing the withdrawal of the UNEF from Egypt. Thus we felt that attempts were being made to turn the UNEF into a force serving neo-imperialism. It is obvious that the UNEF entered Egypt with our approval and therefore cannot continue to stay in Egypt except with our approval. Until yesterday a great deal was said about the UNEF. A campaign is also being mounted against the UN Secretary-General because he made a faithful and honest decision and could not surrender to the pressure brought to bear upon him by the United States, Britain and Canada to make the UNEF an instrument for implementing imperialism's plans.

It is quite natural, and I say this quite frankly, that had the UNEF ignored its basic task and turned to working for the aims of imperialism we would have regarded it as a hostile force and forcibly disarmed it. We are definitely capable of doing such a job. I say this now not to discredit the UNEF but to those who have neo-imperialist ideas and who want the UNEF to achieve their neo-imperialist aims — that there is not a single nation which respects itself and enjoys full sovereignty which would accept these methods in any shape or form. At the same time I say that the UNEF has honourably and faith-fully carried out its duties. The UN Secretary-General refused to succumb to pressure. He issued immediate orders to the UNEF to withdraw. Consequently we praise the UNEF which has stayed ten years in our country serving peace. And when they left — at a time when we found that the neo-imperialist force wanted to divert them from their basic task — we gave them a cheerful send-off and saluted them.

.   .   .

The armed forces' responsibility is now yours. The armed forces yesterday occupied Sharm ash-Shaykh. What does this mean? It is affirmation of our rights and our sovereignty over the Gulf of Aqabah which constitutes Egyptian territorial waters. Under no circumstances will we allow the Israeli flag to pass through the Gulf of Aqabah.

The Jews threaten war. We tell them you are welcome, we are ready for war. Our armed forces and all our people are ready for war, but under no circumstances will we abandon any of our rights. This water is ours. War might be an opportunity for the Jews, for Israel and Rabin, to test their forces against ours and to see that what they wrote about the 1956 battle and the occupation of Sinai was all a lot of nonsense.

SWB, ME/2473/A/1 – 4

59   Speech by Gideon Rafael, Israel, to the Security Council on his country's view of the blockade of the Straits of Tiran, 24 May 1967

. . . massive troop concentrations have been built up in the Sinai peninsula, along the southern borders of Israel. The United Nations Emergency Force, which for ten years has assisted in maintaining stability there, was peremptorily evicted. All these steps were part of an over-all plan, the design of which is now unfolding. It is approaching its culmination in the threats of President Nasser to interfere with shipping in the Straits of Tiran at the entrance to the Gulf of Aqaba. That announcement was made while the Secretary-General of the United Nations was on his way to Cairo on his mission to preserve the peace. Before the Secretary-General had an opportunity to meet President Nasser, it has been reported now from Cairo that Egypt has decided to initiate operational measures to interfere with the freedom of navigation in the international waterway, the Straits of Tiran. According to these reports, these measures include laying mines in the international waterway and opening fire on vessels which do not submit to search.

As the Prime Minister of Israel, Mr Eshkol, stated yesterday in the Knesset, interference with shipping to and from Israel, and the Israel port of Eilat, would be an act of aggression. The Prime Minister said:
   'Every interference with the freedom of navigation in the Gulf of Aqaba and in the Straits of Tiran constitutes a gross violation of international law, an infringement of the sovereign rights of other people and an act of aggression against Israel.'
The Prime Minister continued:
   'From 1957 onwards other Governments, including the main maritime Powers publicly committed themselves to exercise their rights to freedom of navigation in the Straits of Tiran and the Gulf of Aqaba. Indeed what is now being challenged is a solemn and clear-cut international obligation. Its implementation will have a

decisive bearing on international security and law. This is, therefore, a fateful hour, not only for Israel but for the whole world.'

The Prime Minister continued:

'In the face of this situation the Government of Israel will maintain the policy which was enunciated in the General Assembly of the United Nations on 1 March 1957 by the then Foreign Minister of Israel, Mrs Golda Meir.'

Mrs Meir stated on that occasion:

'The Gulf of Aqaba comprehends international waters and . . . no nation has the right to prevent free and innocent passage in the Gulf and through the Straits giving access thereto, in accordance with the generally accepted definition of those terms in the law of the sea.'

(A/PV. 666, para. 11)

That statement continues:

'Israel is resolved on behalf of vessels of Israel registry to exercise the right of free and innocent passage and is prepared to join with others to secure universal respect of this right. Israel will protect ships of its own flag exercising the right of free and innocent passage on the high seas and in international waters.'

'Interference, by armed force, with ships of Israel flag exercising free and innocent passage in the Gulf of Aqaba and through the Straits of Tiran, will be regarded by Israel as an attack entitling it to exercise its inherent right of self-defence under Article 51 of the United Nations Charter and to take all such measures as are necessary to ensure the free and innocent passage of its ships in the Gulf and in the Straits.'

(Ibid., paras. 12 and 13)

The Prime Minister continued in his statement to the Knesset yesterday:

'Since that statement was made free passage in the Straits and in the Gulf of Aqaba has been an established international reality which has been sustained for ten years by hundreds of sailings under a great number of different flags, including the Israeli flag and by the establishment of a wide and expanding pattern of trade and communications. The illegal proclamation by the President of the United Arab Republic to close the Straits of Tiran is another violation by Egypt of international law in addition to the long-standing illegal blockade of the Suez Canal which Egypt maintains in defiance of its international obligations and the resolution of the Security Council of 1 September 1951.'

UNO SCOR, S/PV. 1349

60   Speech by Mohammed Awad El-Kony, Egypt, to the Security Council on his country's reasons for the blockade of the Straits of Tiran, 29 May 1967

As the members of the Council are well aware the Gulf of Aqaba is a long narrow gulf on the eastern side of the Sinai Peninsula. The length of the Gulf is about ninety-six miles and the widest breadth less than fifteen miles. The entrance to the Gulf is situated in the joint territorial waters of Saudi Arabia and the United Arab Republic. Due to navigational hazards the only navigable route to the Gulf runs less than one mile from the Sinai Peninsula. Hence, it crosses our undisputed territorial waters.

The Israelis claim that they have the right to navigate in the Gulf. This we proclaim is without foundation. a cogent reply which refutes the allegation of the Israelis rests on the following facts:

Historically, the Gulf has been under continued and uninterrupted Arab domination for over one thousand years. It always has been a national inland waterway subject to absolute Arab sovereignty. Its geographical location is conclusive proof of its national character. By its configuration it has a nature of a *mare clausum* which does not belong to the class of international waterways. . . .

It certainly will be argued that the Israelis have a port on the Gulf. But even that presence lacks legitimate foundation.

The Israeli armed forces on 10 March 1949 usurped and occupied the village of Om Rashrash, along with a stretch of about five miles overlooking the Gulf of Aqaba. . . . This illegal act was perpetrated two weeks after the signing of the Egyptian-Israeli General Armistice Agreement on 24 February 1949.

UNO SCOR, S/PV. 1343

61   President Nasser's speech to Egyptian National Assembly Members, 29 May 1967

Preparations have already been made, We are now ready to confront Israel. They have claimed many things about the 1956 Suez war, but no one believed them after the secrets of the 1956 collusion were uncovered — that mean collusion in which Israel took part. Now we are ready for the confrontation. We are now ready to deal with the entire Palestine question.

The issue now at hand is not the Gulf of Aqabah, the Straits of

Tiran, or the withdrawal of the UNEF, but the rights of the Palestine people. It is the aggression which took place in Palestine in 1948 with the collaboration of Britain and the United States. It is the expulsion of the Arabs from Palestine, the usurpation of their rights, and the plunder of their property. It is the disavowal of all the UN resolutions in favour of the Palestinian people.

The issue today is far more serious than they say. They want to confine the issue to the Straits of Tiran, the UNEF and the right of passage. We demand the full rights of the Palestinian people. We say this out of our belief that Arab rights cannot be squandered because the Arabs throughout the Arab world are demanding these Arab rights.

We are not afraid of the United States and its threats, of Britain and her threats, or of the entire Western world and its partiality to Israel. The United States and Britain are partial to Israel and give no consideration to the Arabs, to the entire Arab nation. Why? Because we have made them believe that we cannot distinguish between friend and foe. We must make them know that we know who our foes are and who our friends are and treat them accordingly.

If the United States and Britain are partial to Israel, we must say that our enemy is not only Israel but also the United States and Britain and treat them as such. If the Western Powers disavow our rights and ridicule and despise us, we Arabs must teach them to respect us and take us seriously. Otherwise all our talk about Palestine, the Palestine people, and Palestinian rights will be null and void and of no consequence. We must treat our enemies as enemies and friends as friends.

SWB, ME/2478/A/14

62 Speech by Abba Eban, Israeli Foreign Minister, to the Security Council on Israel's reasons for going to war, 6 June 1967

I thank you, Mr President, for giving me this opportunity to address the Council. I have just come from Jerusalem to tell the Security Council that Israel, by its independent action and sacrifice, has passed from serious danger to successful resistance.

Two days ago, Israel's condition caused much concern across the humane and friendly world. Israel had reached a sombre hour. Let me try to evoke the point at which our fortunes stood.

An army, greater than any force ever assembled in history in Sinai, had massed against Israel's southern frontier. Egypt had dismissed the United Nations forces which symbolized the international interest in the maintenance of peace in our region. Nasser had provocatively brought five infantry divisions and two armoured divisions up to our very gates; 80,000 men and 900 tanks were poised to move.

A special striking force, comprising an armoured division with at least 200 tanks, was concentrated against Elath at the Negev's southern tip. Here was a clear design to cut the southern Negev off from the main body of our State. For Egypt had openly proclaimed that Elath did not form part of Israel and had predicted that Israel itself would soon expire. The proclamation was empty; the prediction now lies in ruins. While the main brunt of the hostile threat was focused on the southern front, an alarming plan of encirclement was under way. With Egypt's initiative and guidance, Israel was already being strangled in its maritime approaches to the whole eastern half of the world. For sixteen years, Israel had been illictly denied passage in the Suez Canal, despite this Security Council's resolution of 1 September 1951. And now the creative enterprise of patient years which had opened an international route across the Strait of Tiran and the Gulf of Aqaba had been suddenly and arbitrarily choked. Israel was and is breathing with only a single lung.

Jordan had been intimidated, against its better interest, into joining a defence pact. It is not a defence pact at all: it is an aggressive pact, of which I saw the consequences with my own eyes yesterday in the shells falling upon institutions of health and culture in the City of Jerusalem. Every house and street in Jerusalem now came into the range of fire as a result of Jordan's adherence to this pact; so also did the crowded, and pathetically narrow coastal strip in which so much of Israel's life and population is concentrated.

Iraqi troops reinforced Jordanian units in areas immediately facing vital and vulnerable Israeli communication centres. Expeditionary forces from Algeria and Kuwait had reached Egyptian territory. Nearly all the Egyptian forces which had been attempting the conquest of the Yemen had been transferred to the coming assault upon Israel. Syrian units, including artillery, overlooked Israeli villages in the Jordan Valley. Terrorist groups came regularly into our territory to kill, plunder and set off explosives, the most recent occasion was five days ago.

In short, there was peril for Israel wherever it looked. Its manpower had been hastily mobilized. Its economy and commerce were beating with feeble pulses. Its streets were dark and empty. There was an apocalyptic air of approaching peril. And Israel faced this danger alone.

We were buoyed up by an unforgettable surge of public sympathy across the world. The friendly Governments expressed the rather ominous hope that Israel would manage to live, but the dominant theme of our condition was danger and solitude.

Now there could be doubt what was intended for us. I heard President Nasser's speech on 26 May. He said:

'We intend to open a general assault against Israel. This will be total war. Our basic aim is the destruction of Israel.'

On 2 June, the Egyptian Commander-in-Chief in Sinai, General Murtagi, published his order of the day, calling on his troops to wage a war of destruction against Israel. Here, then, was a systematic, overt, proclaimed design at politicide, the murder of a State.

The policy, the arms, the men had all been brought together, and the State thus threatened with collective assault was itself the last sanctuary of a people which had seen six million of its sons exterminated by a more powerful dictator two decades before.

UNO SCOR, S/PV, 1348

63   President Nasser's broadcast of 9 June 1967

All of us know how the crisis started in the Middle East. At the beginning of last May there was an enemy plan for the invasion of Syria and the statements by his politicians and all his military leaders openly said so. There was plenty of evidence concerning the plan. Sources of our Syrian brothers were categorical on this and our own reliable information confirmed it. Add to this the fact that our friends in the Soviet Union warned the parliamentary delegation, which was on a visit to Moscow, at the beginning of last month, that there was a premeditated plot against Syria. We considered it our duty not to accept this silently. This was the duty of Arab brotherhood, it was also the duty of national security. Whoever starts with Syria will finish with Egypt.

Our armed forces moved to our frontiers with a competence which the enemy acknowledged even before our friends. Several steps followed. There was the withdrawal of the United Nations Emergency Force and the return of our forces to the Sharm ash-Shaykh post, the controlling point in the Straits of Tiran, which had been used by the Israeli enemy as one of the after effects of the tripartite aggression against it in 1956. The enemy's flag passing in front of our forces was intolerable, apart from other reasons connected with the dearest aspirations of the Arab nation.

Accurate calculations were made of the enemy's strength and showed us that our armed forces, at the level of equipment and training which they had reached, were capable of repelling the enemy and deterring him. We realized the possibility of an armed clash and accepted the risk.

.   .   .

In the morning of last Monday, 5 June, the enemy struck. If we say now it was a stronger blow than we had expected, we must say at the same time, and with complete certainty that it was bigger than the potential at his disposal. It became very clear from the first moment that there were other powers behind the enemy — they came to settle their accounts with the Arab national movement.

.   .   .

We now have several urgent tasks before us. The first is to remove the traces of this aggression against us and to stand by the Arab nation resolutely and firmly; despite the setback, the Arab nation, with all its potential and resources, is in a position to insist on the removal of the traces of the aggression.

The second task is to learn the lesson of the setback. In this connection there are three vital facts. (1) The elimination of imperialism in the Arab world will leave Israel with its own intrinsic power; yet, whatever the circumstances, however long it may take the Arab intrinsic power is greater and more effective. (2) Redirecting Arab interests in the service of Arab rights is an essential safeguard: the American Sixth Fleet moved with Arab oil, and there are Arab bases, placed forcibly and against the will of the peoples, in the service of aggression. (3) The situation now demands a united word from the entire Arab nation: this, in the present circumstances, is irreplaceable guarantee.

Now we arrive at an important point in this heartsearching by asking ourselves: does this mean that we do not bear responsibility for the consequences of the setback? I tell you truthfully and despite any factors on which I might have based my attitude during the crisis, that I am ready to bear the whole responsibility. I have taken a decision in which I want you all to help me. I have decided to give up completely and finally every official post and every political role and to return to the ranks of the masses and do my duty with them like every other citizen.

.   .   .

In accordance with Article 110 of the Provisional Constitution promulgated in March 1964 I have entrusted my colleague, friend and brother Zakariya Muhyi ad-Din with taking over the post of President and carrying out the constitutional provisions on this point. After this decision, I place all I have at his disposal in dealing with the grave situation through which our people are passing.

SWB, ME/2488/A/1 – 4

VII

New Realities and the Search for a Middle Eastern Peace Settlement

The 1967 war not only tipped the balance of power in the Middle East in Israel's favour, leaving her for the next few years the decisive military factor in the region; the United States, alarmed by the inherent dangers to world stability the conflict had exposed, became intimately involved in the search for some form of peace settlement. President Lyndon Johnson's speech of 19 June 1967 (**64**) reflects both this new concern and the state of Washington's perceptions at this time. Israeli governmental and public opinion was, and remained, divided over the ultimate destiny of the conquered territories on the West Bank, regarded by many as Judea and Samaria, but the country was virtually unanimous in its determination that east Jerusalem, with its powerful religious ties, should be formally annexed. A law to this effect, enacted by the Knesset on 27 June 1967, attracted immediate universal condemnation (**65**) and alienated orthodox Muslims throughout the Arab world.

Arab heads of state met at Khartoum in an attempt to come to terms with the new realities of Israeli power and devise a strategy for the recovery of the lost territories. The apparently uncompromising resolution they adopted (**66**) at least pointed to a desire to work for a political, rather than a military, solution and concealed a degree of willingness to compromise on the part of Egypt and Jordan. Security Council Resolution 242 (**67**), which formed the basis for all subsequent peace negotiations, though drafted by Britain clearly reflects American inspiration (**64**). Its ambiguities, which were to be the bane of diplomats, can be seen in documents **68** and **69**.

The Arab defeat also led to changing perceptions amongst the Palestinians, for whom the war had been an unmitigated calamity (**70**). A belief that only Palestinian efforts could effect a change in their conditions revitalized the PLO, which convened a congress in July 1968 to adopt a new version of its national charter (**71**), an earlier form of which had appeared in 1964. The following year Yasser

Arafat, the Fatah leader, became chairman of the PLO's executive committee. Between 1968 and 1973, several Palestinian guerrilla groups, the most powerful of which were Fatah and Dr George Habash's Popular Front for the Liberation of Palestine, mounted a widespread campaign of violence against Israel, the murder of its athletes during the 1972 Munich Olympics being but the most sensational example. Their escalating guerrilla activity did nothing to soften the negotiating positions of the other parties to the conflict.

Dr Gunnar Jarring, whose thankless task was to work for the implementation of Resolution 242 under United Nations auspices, could make little headway and by April 1969 the United States, with Soviet assistance, had to adopt a more active stance in pushing negotiations forward (72). The plan announced by Secretary of State William Rogers in December 1969 (73), although it proved unacceptable to Israel and Egypt, strikingly revealed the more flexible parameters within which American diplomacy was working. Dr Jarring's final attempt to confront the two major parties with their obligations under Resolution 242 came with the presentation of memoranda (74) to the Egyptian and Israeli governments in February 1971. The previous September Nasser had died suddenly while attempting to mediate between King Hussein of Jordan and Yasser Arafat after the former's assault on PLO bases in his country. The new Egyptian president, Anwar al-Sadat, responded favourably to Jarring's proposals, but the initiative foundered on Israel's refusal to contemplate a return to her pre-1967 frontiers.

64 'Principles for Peace in the Middle East', address by President Lyndon Johnson, 19 June 1967

Now, finally, let me turn to the Middle East — and to the tumultuous events of the past months. Those events have proved the wisdom of five great principles of peace in the region.

The first and greatest principle is that every nation in the area has a fundamental right to live and to have this right respected by its neighbors.

For the people of the Middle East the path to hope does not lie in threats to end the life of any nation. Such threats have become a burden to the peace, not only of that region but a burden to the peace of the entire world.

In the same way, no nation would be true to the United Nations

Charter or to its own true interests if it should permit military success to blind it to the fact that its neighbors have rights and its neighbors have interests of their own. Each nation, therefore, must accept the right of others to live.

This last month, I think, shows us another basic requirement for settlement. It is a human requirement: justice for the refugees.

A new conflict has brought new homelessness. The nations of the Middle East must at last address themselves to the plight of those who have been displaced by wars. In the past, both sides have resisted the best efforts of outside mediators to restore the victims of conflict to their homes or to find them other proper places to live and work. There will be no peace for any party in the Middle East unless this problem is attacked with new energy by all and, certainly, primarily by those who are immediately concerned.

A third lesson from this last month is that maritime rights must be respected. Our nation has long been committed to free maritime passage through international waterways; and we, along with other nations, were taking the necessary steps to implement this principle when hostilities exploded. If a single act of folly was more responsible for this explosion than any other, I think it was the arbitary and dangerous announced decision that the Straits of Tiran would be closed. The right of innocent maritime passage must be preserved for all nations.

Fourth, this last conflict has demonstrated the danger of the Middle East arms race of the last 12 years. Here the responsibility must rest not only on those in the area but upon the larger states outside the area. We believe that scarce resources could be used much better for technical and economic development. We have always opposed this arms race, and our military shipments to the area have consequently been severely limited.

Now the waste and futility of the arms race must be apparent to all the peoples of the world. And now there is another moment of choice. The United States of America, for its part, will use every resource of diplomacy and every counsel of reason and prudence to try to find a better course.

As a beginning, I should like to propose that the United Nations immediately call upon all of its members to report all shipments of all military arms into this area and to keep those shipments on file for all the peoples of the world to observe.

Fifth, the crisis underlines the importance of respect for political independence and territorial integrity of all the states in the area. We reaffirmed that principle at the height of this crisis. We reaffirm it again today on behalf of all. This principle can be effective in the Middle East only on the basis of peace between the parties. The nations of the region have had only fragile and violated truce lines for 20 years. What they now need are recognized boundaries and other arrangements that will give them security against terror, destruction and war. Further, there must be adequate recognition of the special interest of three great religions in the holy places of Jerusalem.

DSB, vol. LVII, no. 1463, 10 July 1969

65   General Assembly resolution on Israeli measures to change the status of the City of Jerusalem, 4 July 1967

The General Assembly,
Deeply concerned at the situation prevailing in Jerusalem as a result of the measures taken by Israel to change the status of the City,
1   *Considers* that these measures are invalid;
2   *Calls upon* Israel to rescind all measures already taken and to desist forthwith from taking any action which would alter the status of Jerusalem;
3   *Requests* the Secretary-General to report to the General Assembly and the Security Council on the situation and on the implementation of the present resolution not later than one week from its adopton.

UNO, doc. A/RES/2253(ES − V)
(A/L527/Rev. 1).

66   Resolutions of the Khartoum conference, 1 September 1967

1   The conference has affirmed the unity of Arab ranks, the unity of joint action and the need for coordination and for the elimination of all differences. The Kings, Presidents and representatives of the other Arab Heads of State at the conference have affirmed their countries' stand by and implementation of the Arab Solidarity Charter which was signed at the third Arab summit conference at Casablanca.
2   The conference has agreed on the need to consolidate all efforts to eliminate the effects of the aggression on the basis that the occupied lands are Arab lands and that the burden of regaining these lands falls on the Arab States.
3   The Arab Heads of State have agreed to unite their political efforts at the international and diplomatic level to eliminate the effects of the

aggression and to ensure the withdrawal of the aggressive Israeli forces from the Arab lands which have been occupied since the aggression of 5 June. This will be done within the framework of the main principles by which the Arab States abide, namely, no peace with Israel, no recognition of Israel, no negotiations with it, and insistence on the rights of the Palestinian people in their own country.

4   The conference of Arab Ministers of Finance, Economy and Oil recommended that suspension of oil pumping be used as a weapon in the battle. However, after thoroughly studying the matter, the summit conference has come to the conclusion that the pumping of oil can itself be used as a positive weapon, since oil is an Arab resource which can be used to strengthen the economy of the Arab States directly affected by the aggression, so that these States will be able to stand firm in the battle. The conference has, therefore, decided to resume the pumping of oil, since oil is a positive Arab resource that can be used in the service of Arab goals. It can contribute to the efforts to enable those Arab States which were exposed to the aggression and thereby lost economic resources to stand firm and eliminate the effects of the aggression.

The oil-producing States have, in fact, participated in the efforts to enable the States affected by the aggression to stand firm in the face of any economic pressure.

5   The participants in the conference have approved the plan proposed by Kuwait to set up an Arab Economic and Social Development Fund on the basis of the recommendations of the Baghdad conference of Arab Ministers of Finance, Economy and Oil.

6   The participants have agreed on the need to adopt the necessary measures to strengthen military preparation to face all eventualities.

7   The conference has decided to expedite the elimination of foreign bases in the Arab States.

.   .   .

The Kingdom of Saudi Arabia, the State of Kuwait and the Kingdom of Libya have each agreed to pay the following annual amounts, which are to be paid in advance every three months beginning from mid-October until the effects of the aggression are eliminated: Saudi Arabia, £50,000,000; Kuwait, £55,000,000; Libya, £30,000,000. In this way, the Arab nation ensures that it will be able to carry on this battle, without any weakening, until the effects of the aggression are eliminated.

SWB, ME/2559/A/1 – 3

67   Security Council Resolution 242, 22 November 1967

The Security Council,

Expressing its continued concern with the grave situation in the Middle East,

Emphasizing the inadmissibility of the acquisition of territory by war and the need to work for a just and lasting peace in which every state in the area can live in security,

Emphasizing further that all Member States in their acceptance of the Charter of the United Nations have undertaken a commitment to act in accordance with Article 2 of the Charter

1   *Affirms* that the fulfilment of Charter principles requires the establishment of a just and lasting peace in the Middle East which should include the application of both the following principles.

(1) Withdrawal of Israel armed forces from territories occupied in the recent conflict;

(2) Termination of all claims or states of belligerency and respect for and acknowledgement of the sovereignty, territorial integrity and political independence of every State in the area and their right to live in peace within secure and recognized boundaries free from threats or acts of force.

2   *Affirms further* the necessity

(*a*) For guaranteeing freedom of navigation through international waterways in the area;

(*b*) For achieving a just settlement of the refugee problem;

(*c*) For guaranteeing the territorial inviolability and political independence of every State in the area, through measures including the establishment of demilitarized zones;

3   *Requests* the Secretary-General to designate a Special Representative to proceed to the Middle East to establish and maintain contacts with the States concerned in order to promote agreement and assist efforts to achieve a peaceful and accepted settlement in accordance with the provisions and principles in this resolution;

4   *Requests* the Secretary-General to report to the Security Council on the progress of the efforts of the Special Representative as soon as possible.

UNO, doc. S/RES/242(1967)

68   Speech by Abba Eban to the Security Council on the Israeli diplomatic stance after Resolution 242, 22 November 1967

The Security Council, like the General Assembly, has constantly refused to endorse principles which would have brought a return to the ambiguity, vulnerability and insecurity in which we have lived for nineteen years. It has now adopted a resolution of which the central and primary affirmation is the need for 'the establishment of a just and lasting peace' based on secure and recognized boundaries. There is a clear understanding that it is only within the establishment of permanent peace with secure and recognized boundaries that the other principles can be given effect. As my delegation and others have stated, the establishment for the first time of agreed and secure boundaries as part of a peace settlement is the only key which can unlock the present situation and set on foot a momentum of con- structive and peaceful progress. As the representative of the United Kingdom indicated in his address of 16 November, the action to be taken must be within the framework of a permanent peace and of secure and recognized boundaries. It has been pointed out in the Security Council, and it is stated in the 1949 agreements, that the armistice demarcation lines have never been recognized as boundaries so that, as the representative of the United States has said, the boundaries between Israel and her neighbours:

' . . . must be mutually worked out and recognized by the parties themselves as part of the peace-making process.' (1377th meeting, pp. 38 – 40)

We continue to believe that the States of the region, in direct negotiation with each other, have the sovereign responsibility for shaping their common future. It is the duty of international agencies at the behest of the parties to act in the measure that agreement can be promoted and a mutually accepted settlement can be advanced. We do not believe that Member States have the right to refuse direct negotiations with those to whom they address their claims. It is only when they come together that the Arab States and Israel will reveal the full potentialities of a peaceful settlement.

UNO, SCOR S/PV.1382

69 Speech by Mahmoud Riad to the Security Council on the Egyptian diplomatic stance after Resolution 242, 22 November 1967

Today, I wish to affirm once again our position that the first step towards peace lies in the full withdrawal of the Israeli forces from all the territories they have occupied as a result of their aggression on 5

June. The efforts on behalf of peace which would then follow would of necessity be within the framework of this Organization and its Charter. The provisions of our Charter prohibit aggression and require all States to assume in good faith their obligations arising from the Charter as well as from international agreements and other sources of international law.

The inalienable rights of the people of Palestine, recognized and continually reaffirmed by the United Nations, belong in the highest and most essential category of the norms and rules of present international order. These rights should under no circumstances be allowed to fall by the wayside. Historically, legally, constitutionally and morally, this Organization is inescapably committed to the rights of the people of Palestine.

UNO, SCOR S/PV.1382

70 The Commissioner-General of the UNRWA on the Palestinian refugees after the 1967 war, 11 December 1967

2 Mr Michelmore (Commissioner-General of the United Nations Relief and Works Agency for Palestine Refugees in the Near East) said that, since the last session of the General Assembly the number of refugees had increased by about 350,000 or 400,000 as a result of the Middle East crisis. Many of the new refugees were dependent on Governments or on the UNRWA or other organizations for food, clothing, medical care and schooling for their children. Those who were still living where they had been before June 1967 were in greater need than before because of the deterioration of the economies in their areas.

3 It was the hope of all that Security Council resolution 242(1967) might mark a turning point in the history of the Middle East. Meanwhile, however, the Palestine refugees must live, and UNRWA must continue its work. It was to be hoped that the very presence of UNRWA in the area would have a beneficial influence and help to remove malaise and uncertainty.

4 The Agency estimated that, counting the 14,000 persons who had returned to the west bank area before 1 September 1967, in accordance with arrangements made by the two Governments concerned and the International Committee of the Red Cross, the total number of displaced persons remaining in east Jordan was now 577,000. To the 332,000 UNRWA refugees living on the east bank before 1 June 1967

must be added 245,000 newly displaced persons; that figure included 111,000 Palestinians formerly registered with UNRWA on the west bank, 120,000 other west bank residents and 15,000 refugees from the Gaza Strip. The Jordanian Government had indicated in addition that some 200 or 300 persons were crossing the River Jordan from west to east daily, the majority of them coming from Gaza.

UNO, GAOR, Twenty-Second Session, Special Political Committee, 584th Meeting, Agenda Item 34, Report of the Commissioner-General of the United Nations Relief and Works Agency for Palestine Refugees in the Near East

71   The Palestinian National Charter, July 1968

1   Palestine is the homeland of the Palestinian Arab people; it is an indivisible part of the Arab homeland, and the Palestinian people are an integral part of the Arab nation.

2   Palestine, with the boundaries it had during the British mandate, is an indivisible territorial unit.

3   The Palestinian Arab people possess the legal right to their homeland and have the right to determine their destiny after achieving the liberation of their country in accordance with their wishes and entirely of their own accord and will.

4   The Palestinian identity is a genuine, essential and inherent characteristic; it is transmitted from parents to children. The Zionist occupation and the dispersal of the Palestinian Arab people, through the disasters which befell them, do not make them lose their Palestinian identity and their membership of the Palestinian community, nor do they negate them.

5   The Palestinians are those Arab nationals who, until 1947, normally resided in Palestine regardless of whether they were evicted from it or have stayed there. Anyone born, after that date, of a Palestinian father — whether inside Palestine or outside it — is also a Palestinian.

6   The Jews who had normally resided in Palestine until the beginning of the Zionist invasion will be considered Palestinians.

.   .   .

9   Armed struggle is the only way to liberate Palestine. Thus it is the overall strategy, not merely a tactical phase. The Palestinian Arab people assert their absolute determination and firm resolution to continue their armed struggle and to work for an armed popular revolution for the liberation of their country and their return to it. They also assert their right to normal life in Palestine and to exercise their right to self-determination and sovereignty over it.

10   Commando action constitutes the nucleus of the Palestinian popular liberation war. This requires its escalation, comprehensiveness and the mobilization of all the Palestinian popular and educational efforts and their organization and involvement in the armed Palestinian revolution. It also requires the achieving of unity for the national struggle among the different groupings of the Palestinian people and the Arab masses so as to secure the continuation of the revolution, its escalation and victory.

.   .   .

12   The Palestinian people believe in Arab unity. In order to contribute their share towards the attainment of that objective, however, they must, at the present stage of their struggle, safeguard their Palestinian identity and develop their consciousness of that identity, and oppose any plan that may dissolve or impair it.

.   .   .

15   The liberation of Palestine, from an Arab viewpoint, is a national duty and it attempts to repel the Zionist and imperialist aggression against the Arab homeland, and aims at the elimination of Zionism in Palestine. Absolute responsibility for this falls upon the Arab nation — peoples and governments — with the Arab people of Palestine in the vanguard. Accordingly the Arab nation must mobilize all its military, human, moral and spiritual capabilities to participate actively with the Palestinian people in the liberation of Palestine. It must, particularly in the phase of the armed Palestinian revolution, offer and furnish the Palestinian people with all possible help, and material and human support, and make available to them the means and opportunities that will enable them to continue to carry out their leading role in the armed revolution, until they liberate their homeland.

.   .   .

19   The partition of Palestine in 1947 and the establishment of the state of Israel are entirely illegal, regardless of the passage of time, because they were contrary to the will of the Palestinian people and their natural right in their homeland, and inconsistent with the principles embodied in the Charter of the United Nations, particularly the right to self-determination.

20   The Balfour Declaration, the mandate for Palestine and everything that has been based upon them, are deemed null and void. Claims of historical or religious ties of Jews with Palestine are incompatible with the facts of history and the true conception of what constitutes statehood. Judaism, being a religion, is not an independent nationality. Nor do Jews constitute a single nation with an identity of its own; they are citizens of the states to which they belong.

.   .   .

22   Zionism is a political movement organically associated with international imperialism and antagonistic to all action for liberation and to progressive movements in the world. It is racist and fanatic in its nature, aggressive, expansionist and colonial in its aims, and fascist in its methods. Israel is the instrument of the Zionist movement, and a geographical base for world imperialism placed strategically in the midst of the Arab homeland to combat the hopes of the Arab nation for liberation, unity and progress. Israel is a constant source of threat *vis-à-vis* peace in the Middle East and the whole world. Since the liberation of Palestine will destroy the Zionist and imperialist presence and will contribute to the establishment of peace in the Middle East, the Palestinian people look for the support of all the progressive and peaceful forces and urge them all, irrespective of their affiliations and beliefs, to offer the Palestinian people all aid and support in their just struggle for the liberation of their homeland.

72   Statement by Secretary of State William Rogers before the Senate Committee on Foreign Relations, 27 March 1969

Finally, what is the mechanism for realizing the principles and provisions of the Security Council resolution? In its third paragraph, the resolution asked the Secretary-General of the United Nations to designate a representative to promote agreement and assist in efforts to achieve a peaceful and acceptable settlement. That representative, to whose patient competence I wish to pay special tribute this morning, is Ambassador Jarring of Sweden. His mission is to promote agreement—and this can only mean agreement between the parties and among the parties. We lay stress on this point because we do not believe that a peace settlement to which the parties did not agree would be just or lasting or, for that matter, attainable at all. We, for our part, are not interested in imposing a peace.

Regrettably, in the 22 months since the war Ambassador Jarring and the parties have not made significant progress. In these circumstances, we are convinced that the United States has a responsibility to help. Our interests would be ill served in the absence of a settlement. Furthermore, we and the other permanent members of the Security Council were instrumental in forging the 1967 resolution which created the mission of Ambassador Jarring. Historically, the United States has played a special role in helping shape the political evolution of the Middle East.

For all these reasons, we have concluded that the United States should play an active role, bilaterally and multilaterally, in support of the United Nations effort. We are therefore actively engaged diplomatically with the other major powers and in particular with the other permanent members of the Security Council, as well as with the principal parties in the area, in efforts to help Ambassador Jarring accomplish his mission. If there is a genuine will to peace on the part of those directly concerned, we believe that the just rights and legitimate security of all the states and peoples in the Middle East can be realized. In the interests of friendly relations with all states in that area, we shall work to that end in the days ahead.

DSB, vol. LX, no. 1555, 14 April 1969

73 Address by Secretary of State William Rogers, 'A Lasting Peace in the Middle East: An American View', 9 December 1969

In an effort to broaden the scope of discussion we have recently resumed four-power negotiations at the United Nations.

Let me outline our policy on various elements of the Security Council resolution. The basic and related issues might be described as peace, security, withdrawal, and territory.

PEACE BETWEEN THE PARTIES

The resolution of the Security Council makes clear that the goal is the establishment of a state of peace between the parties instead of the state of belligerency which has characterized relations for over 20 years. We believe the conditions and obligations of peace must be defined in specific terms. For example, navigation rights in the Suez Canal and in the Straits of Tiran should be spelled out. Respect for sovereignty and obligations of the parties to each other must be made specific.

But peace, of course, involves much more than this. It is also a matter of the attitudes and intentions of the parties. Are they ready to coexist with one another? Can a live-and-let-live attitude replace suspicion, mistrust, and hate? A peace agreement between the parties must be based on clear and stated intentions and a willingness to bring about basic changes in the attitudes and conditions which are characteristic of the Middle East today.

SECURITY

A lasting peace must be sustained by a sense of security on both sides. To this end, as envisaged in the Security Council resolution, there should be demilitarized zones and related security arrangements more reliable than those which existed in the area in the past. The parties themselves, with Ambassador Jarring's help, are in the best position to work out the nature and the details of such security arrangements. It is, after all, their interests which are at stake and their territory which is involved. They must live with the results.

WITHDRAWAL AND TERRITORY

The Security Council resolution endorses the principle of the non-acquisition of territory by war and calls for withdrawal of Israeli armed forces from territories occupied in the 1967 war. We support this part of the resolution, including withdrawal, just as we do its other elements.

The boundaries from which the 1967 war began were established in the 1949 armistice agreements and have defined the areas of national jurisdiction in the Middle East for 20 years. These boundaries were armistice lines, not final political borders. The rights, claims, and positions of the parties in an ultimate peaceful settlement were reserved by the armistice agreements.

The Security Council resolution neither endorses nor precludes these armistice lines as the definitive political boundaries. However, it calls for withdrawal from occupied territories, the nonacquisition of territory by war, and the establishment of secure and recognized boundaries.

We believe that while recognized political boundaries must be established, and agreed upon by the parties, any changes in the pre-existing lines should not reflect the weight of conquest and should be confined to insubstantial alterations required for mutual security. We do not support expansionism. We believe troops must be withdrawn as the resolution provides. We support Israel's security and the security of the Arab states as well. We are for a lasting peace that requires security for both.

ISSUES OF REFUGEES AND JERUSALEM

By emphasizing the key issues of peace, security, withdrawal, and territory, I do not want to leave the impression that other issues are not equally important. Two in particular deserve special mention: the questions of refugees and of Jerusalem.

There can be no lasting peace without a just settlement of the problem of those Palestinians whom the wars of 1948 and 1967 have made homeless. This human dimension of the Arab-Israeli conflict has been of special concern to the United States for over 20 years. During this period the United States has contributed about $500 million for the support and education of the Palestine refugees. We are prepared to contribute generously along with others to solve this problem. We believe its just settlement must take into account the desires and aspirations of the refugees and the legitimate concerns of the governments in the area.

The problem posed by the refugees will become increasingly serious if their future is not resolved. There is a new consciousness among the young Palestinians who have grown up since 1948 which needs to be channelled away from bitterness and frustration toward hope and justice.

The question of the future status of Jerusalem, because it touches deep emotional, historical, and religious wellsprings, is particularly complicated. We have made clear repeatedly in the past two and a half years that we cannot accept unilateral actions by any party to decide the final status of the city. We believe its status can be determined only through the agreement of the parties concerned, which in practical terms means primarily the Governments of Israel and Jordan, taking into account the interests of other countries in the area and the international community. We do, however, support certain principles which we believe would provide an equitable framework for a Jerusalem settlement.

Specifically, we believe Jerusalem should be a unified city within which there would no longer be restrictions on the movement of persons and goods. There should be open access to the unified city for persons of all faiths and nationalities. Arrangements for the administration of the unified city should take into account the interests of all its inhabitants and of the Jewish, Islamic, and Christian communities. And there should be roles for both Israel and Jordan in the civic, economic, and religious life of the city.

It is our hope that agreement on the key issues of peace, security, withdrawal and territory, will create a climate in which these questions of refugees and of Jerusalem, as well as other aspects of the conflict, can be resolved as part of the overall settlement.

DSB, vol. LXII, no. 1593, 4 January 1970

74 Aide-mémoire presented to Israel and Egypt by Ambassador Gunnar Jarring, 8 February 1971

I have been following with a mixture of restrained optimism and growing concern the resumed discussions under my auspices for the purpose of arriving at a peaceful settlement of the Middle East question. My restrained optimism arises from the fact that in my view the parties are seriously devining their positions and wish to move forward to a permanent peace. My growing concern is that each side unyieldingly insists that the other make certain commitments before being ready to proceed to the stage of formulating the provisions to be included in a final peace agreement. There is, as I see it, a serious risk that we shall find ourselves in the same deadlock that existed during the first three years of my mission.

I therefore feel that I should at this stage make clear my views on what I believe to be the necessary steps to be taken in order to achieve a peaceful and accepted settlement in accordance with the provisions and principles of Security Council resolution 242(1967), which the parties have agreed to carry out in all its parts.

I have come to the conclusion that the only possibility to break the imminent deadlock arising from the differing views of Israel and the United Arab Republic as to the priority to be given to commitments and undertakings—which seems to me to be the real cause of the present immobility—is for me to seek from each side the parallel and simultaneous commitments which seem to be inevitable prerequisites of an eventual peace settlement between them. It should thereafter be possible to proceed at once to formulate the provisions and terms of a peace agreement not only for those topics covered by the commitments, but with equal priority for other topics, and in particular the refugee question.

Specifically, I wish to request the Governments of Israel and the United Arab Republic to make to me at this stage the following prior commitments simultaneously and on condition that the other party makes its commitments and subject to the eventual satisfactory determination of all other aspects of a peace settlement, including in particular a just settlement of the refugee problem.

1   ISRAEL

Israel would give a commitment to withdraw its forces from occupied United Arab Republic territory to the former international boundary between Egypt and the British Mandate of Palestine on the understanding that satisfactory arrangements are made for:

(a) Establishing demilitarized zones;

(b) Practical security arrangements in the Sharm el Sheikh area for guaranteeing freedom of navigation through the Straits of Tiran;

(c) Freedom of navigation through the Suez Canal.

2   UNITED ARAB REPUBLIC

The United Arab Republic would give a commitment to enter into a peace agreement with Israel and to make explicitly therein to Israel, on a reciprocal basis, undertakings and acknowledgements covering the following subjects:

(a) Termination of all claims or states of belligerency;

(b) Respect for and acknowledgement of each other's sovereignty, territorial integrity and political independence;

(c) Respect for and acknowledgement of each other's right to live in peace within secure and recognized boundaries;

(d) Responsibility to do all in their power to ensure that acts of belligerency or hostility do not originate from or are not committed from within their respective territories against the population, citizens or property of the other party;

(e) Non-interference in each other's domestic affairs.

In making the above-mentioned suggestion I am conscious that I am requesting both sides to make serious commitments but I am convinced that the present situtation requires me to take this step.

UNO, *The Origins and Evolution of the Palestine Problem,* Part II: 1947 – 1977, Annex V

VIII

The October War

The failure of Rogers and Jarring to make any advance from Resolution 242 seemed to confirm that Arab-Israeli relations were again set for stalemate, but once President Sadat felt that his grip on Egyptian affairs was secure, he initiated two bold foreign-policy gambits which be believed would help free the situation. The first came in October 1972 when he announced the expulsion of the Soviet military personnel on whom his predecessor had come increasingly to depend; the second was the war which he launched in conjunction with the Syrians in October the following year.

On 6 October 1973, the fourth Arab-Israeli war began with a massive Syrian armoured assault on the Golan front and a successful Egyptian crossing of the Suez Canal. Despite the fact that in the shock of initial defeat the Israeli government understandably characterized the war as one of extermination against their state, Arab war aims, at least those of President Sadat, were limited. By the final cease-fire on 25 October, the Israelis had succeeded in holding both offensives, even gaining territory in Syria and on the west bank of the Suez Canal. But the fighting had cost them serious casualties and the Egyptians had not been dislodged from their new positions in Sinai. On 16 October, President Sadat publicly defined his war aims in terms of a peace settlement to include an Israeli withdrawal to her pre-1967 borders and respect for Palestinian rights (75), points which were to be re-emphasized at the Algiers Arab summit held in late November (79). Moves towards a general Middle Eastern peace settlement were also anticipated in Security Council Resolution 338 (76), which set the terms of the final cease-fire.

The ramifications of the war were felt far beyond the Middle East. This was especially true of the international oil crisis which it exacerbated, but which will be examined at some length in section XI. The prospect of Soviet military intervention on behalf of the Arabs triggered an American nuclear alert which took effect at midnight on

24/25 October, producing the most dramatic incident between the superpowers since the Cuban crisis of 1962 (**77**). Despite Israel's successes towards the end of the war, she could no longer take refuge behind the myth of her perennial military superiority in the region, and Syria and Egypt could take a new pride in the achievements of their soldiers (**78**).

75   President Sadat's address to the People's Assembly, 16 October 1973

Brothers and sisters, I have thought of sending President Richard Nixon a letter in which I would clearly define our position. But I hesitated lest this might be misinterpreted. For this reason, I have decided instead to address an open message to him from here. This is a message dictated not by fear but by confidence. It is a message that emanates not from weakness but from a genuine desire to protect peace and bolster detente. I wish to tell him clearly that our aim in the war is well known and there is no need for us to explain it again. If you want to know our terms for peace, then here is our peace plan:

1   We have fought and will fight to liberate our territories which the Israeli occupation seized in 1967 and to find a means to retrieve and secure respect for the legitimate rights of the Palestinian people. In this respect, we uphold our commitment to the UN resolutions, (those of) the General Assembly and the Security Council.

2   We are prepared to accept a cease-fire on the basis of the immediate withdrawal of the Israeli forces from all the occupied territories, under international supervision, to the pre-5th June 1967 lines.

3   We are prepared, as soon as the withdrawal from all these territories has been completed, to attend an international peace conference at the United Nations, which I will try my best to persuade my comrades, the Arab leaders directly responsible for running our conflict with the enemy (to accept). I will also do my best to convince the Palestine people's representatives about this so that they may participate with us and with the assembled states in laying down rules and regulations for a peace in the area based on the respect of the legitimate rights of all the peoples of the area.

4   We are ready at this hour — indeed at this very moment — to begin clearing the Suez Canal and to open it for world navigation so that it may resume its role in serving world prosperity and welfare. I have actually issued an order to the head of the Suez Canal Authority to

begin this operation on the day following the liberation of the eastern
bank of the Canal. Preliminary preparations for this operation have
already begun.

5   In all this, we are not prepared to accept any ambiguous promises
or loose words which can be given all sorts of interpretations and only
waste time in useless things and put our cause back to the state of
inaction, which we no longer accept whatever reasons the others may
have or whatever sacrifices we have to make. What we want now is
clarity: clarity of aims and clarity of means.

SWB, ME/4427/A/7 – 9

76   Security Council Resolution 338, 22 October 1973

The Security Council,

1   *Calls upon* all parties to the present fighting to cease all firing and
terminate all military activity immediately, not later than 12 hours
after the moment of the adoption of the decision, in the positions they
now occupy;

2   *Calls upon* the parties concerned to start immediately after the
ceasefire the implementation of Security Council Resolution 242
(1967) in all of its parts;

3   *Decides that*, immediately and concurrently with the ceasefire
negotiations start between the parties concerned under appropriate
auspices aimed at establishing a just and durable peace in the Middle
East.

UNO, UN doc. PR/73/29 (1973)

77   President Richard Nixon's news conference, 26 October 1973

The cease-fire is holding. There have been some violations, but
generally speaking, it can be said that it is holding at this time. As you
know, as a result of the UN resolution which was agreed to yesterday by
a vote of 14 to 0, a peacekeeping force will go to the Mideast; and this
force, however, will not include any forces from the major powers,
including, of course, the United States and the Soviet Union.

The question, however, has arisen as to whether observers from
major powers could go to the Mideast. My up-to-the-minute report on
that — and I just talked to Dr Kissinger five minutes before coming
down — is this. We will send observers to the Mideast if requested by

the Secretary-General of the United Nations, and we have reason to expect that we will receive such a request.

With regard to the peacekeeping force, I think it is important for all of you ladies and gentlemen, and particularly for those listening on radio and television, to know why the United States has insisted that major powers not be part of the peacekeeping force and that major powers not introduce military forces into the Mideast. A very significant and potentially explosive crisis developed on Wednesday of this week. We obtained information which led us to believe that the Soviet Union was planning to send a very substantial force into the Mideast, a military force.

When I received that information, I ordered, shortly after midnight on Thursday morning, an alert for all American forces around the world. This was a precautionary alert. The purpose of that was to indicate to the Soviet Union that we could not accept any unilateral move on their part to move military forces into the Mideast.

At the same time, in the early morning hours, I also proceeded on the diplomatic front. In a message to Mr Brezhnev [Leonid I. Brezhnev, General Secretary of the Soviet Communist Party], an urgent message, I indicated to him our reasoning and I urged that we not proceed along that course and that, instead, that we join in the United Nations in supporting a resolution which would exclude any major powers from participating in a peacekeeping force.

As a result of that communication and the return that I received from Mr Brezhnev — we had several exchanges, I should say — we reached the conclusion that we would jointly support the resolution which was adopted in the United Nations.

DSB, vol. LXIX, no. 1794, 12
November 1973

78   Address by President Hafiz al-Assad of Syria, 29 October 1973

Brothers, the victories we scored during this war are illustrious victories that our history will proudly record. They deserve appreciation and admiration from all of us. They have added to our nation's glorious history illustrious and glorious pages. They are among the most brilliant achievements made by our people during their struggle of this age.

What do these victories mean? Do they mean that we have liberated the territories occupied by the enemy? No, we have not yet liberated the territories. In fact, some of the land in the penetrated area is still in enemy hands, because the cease-fire came as a surprise to us and contrary to the picture we had about the course of the battle. We had in mind a long-term battle. In such a case, our moves take different directions and are characterized by great flexibility to serve the ultimate objective of the battle. Within this picture, too, it might not be harmful but could be useful to us if the enemy had been here or there, in a near or distant area, for a period of time which could be brief or long. All that and other things would be done in the light of a clear-cut guide — the ultimate objective of the war.

Undoubtedly, the fraternal citizens now listening to me would wish for more explanation of this particular point. More explanation and details, however, could benefit the enemy. I, too, would like to talk more about this point but I am prevented from doing so by the possible benefit to the enemy. Hence, I say again that we have not yet liberated the territories, that the Security Council resolution took us by surprise and was contrary to our course and to the picture we had in mind.

What then are our victories? They are great. We have not liberated the territories but we have liberated the essential thing leading to that — things which had to be liberated first. We have liberated our will from all fetters. We have liberated our will to fight for an honourable and dignified life. We have liberated our spirits from fear, hesitation and indifference. We have freed our souls from the complex of guilt and failure, since in the past and ever since the establishment of Israel we never fought as we should have fought.

We have liberated our true image from all falsehood and distortion. It is now an image that proves our ability to absorb and make use of the battles. It is an image that proves our great ability in the field of science and our ability to make use of its data and results. It is an image that proves that there are many big talents in our nation. It is an image that we believe in what is right and strongly defend what we believe in. It is an image that stresses that we reject defeatism and that there is no place for cowards among us.

We have liberated our true image from all falsehood and distortion. It is now an image that represents redemption, sacrifice and heroism. These are the things we have realized. These are our victories. They are definitely a starting-point and a basis for other victories. These victories are a large and permanent asset for our people and nation. No victory can be scored under ignorance, fear, hesitation or defeatism. It was, therefore, essential that we should first triumph against ignorance, fear, hesitation and defeatism and then go ahead to triumph in any battle we wage to realize any of our aims.

SWB, ME/4438/A/7 – 12

79 Declaration of the Algiers Arab Summit, 28 November 1973

The cease-fire is not peace. Peace requires a number of conditions, in the forefront of which two are basic and immutable. These are: (1) the withdrawal of Israel from all the Arab occupied territories, and first and foremost from Jerusalem; (2) the restoration to the Palestinian people of their established national rights.

So long as these two conditions are not met it is a delusion to expect anything to happen in the Middle East except an aggravation of the explosive circumstances and renewed confrontation.

The Arab kings and presidents, out of their realization of their historic responsibilities, reaffirm their readiness to participate in bringing about a just peace on the basis of the two above-mentioned conditions. As to those who speak about peace, it is up to them to prove with actions their desire to put an end to a situation which every day becomes more dangerous and explosive.

The Arab countries will in no circumstances agree to make their future subject to vague promises and misleading bargains. World public opinion should not allow itself to entertain the slightest doubt—having been constantly deceived by Zionist propaganda—about the determination and will of the Arab nation to effect the restoration of its usurped rights and the liberation of its occupied territories. Peace cannot be brought about except through complete clarity and by avoidance of manoeuvres and deception and on the basis of the principles set forth in this declaration. For this reason the Arab kings and presidents declare that any serious and constructive consultations must be conducted within this framework.

Should the conditions needed to bring about a just peace be unavailable and should the Arab efforts to bring about peace be rejected by Israel and its allies, then the Arab states will find themselves compelled to draw the natural conclusions and continue their battle of liberation, however long this may last, using all the means in the various fields.

In conclusion, the political declaration issued by the meeting of the Arab kings and presidents stated: The Arab nation, which is determined to do its duty, is prepared for further struggle and sacrifice. It is up to the whole world to bear its responsibility to halt the aggression and to support the just Arab struggle.

SWB, ME/4464/A/1 – 3

IX

The Aftermath of War

The twelve months after the October war saw the PLO enhance its status in the Arab world and beyond, gaining for it a diplomatic position of some substance. At Rabat in October 1974, the Arab heads of state recognized it as the sole legitimate representative of the Palestinian people (80). The following month, Yasser Arafat achieved a considerable personal triumph when he was invited to address the United Nations General Assembly on his organization's behalf. In opposing this gesture (82), Israel's delegate castigated the PLO for the acts of violence which had accompanied its rise and attempted to set the Palestinian problem within a Jordanian context. Arafat's speech (81) was a major effort to justify the nature of his movement's struggle and explain its aspirations, the fruits of which can be seen in the subsequent General Assembly resolution (83). With the outbreak in 1975 of the Lebanese civil war, which its activities had helped provoke and which increasingly absorbed its efforts, the PLO's general influence in the Middle East failed to develop from this high point. Even so, as its diplomatic contacts were to reveal, it had become a significant voice in international affairs.

As President Sadat had long hoped, the war impelled the United States to exert its powerful diplomatic influence on behalf of a resolution of Arab-Israeli differences. After arduous negotiations, in September 1975 Secretary of State Henry Kissinger secured acceptance of a disengagement agreement for Sinai which marked a decisive development in relations between Egypt and Israel (84, **Map 3**). Not only did Israel make the important military concession of withdrawal behind the strategic Gidi and Mitla passes but Egypt was now prepared to allow non-military Israeli cargoes through the Suez Canal. Moreover, both parties looked forward to active negotiations for a peace settlement. Document **85** gives Dr Kissinger's definition of America's Middle Eastern policy, emphasizing both a continuing commitment to Israel along with the need to take account of Arab oil power. The harmonious working of the Sinai agreement undoubtedly helped cultivate the spirit of mutual confidence needed for progress towards a more far-reaching settlement, but the grudging nature of the subsequent Geneva peace talks showed that formidable obstacles remained.

80   Resolution of the Rabat Arab summit, 28 October 1974

The Conference of the Arab Heads of State:
1   *Affirms* the right of the Palestinian people to return to their home-land and to self-determination.
2   *Affirms* the right of the Palestinian people to establish an independent national authority, under the leadership of the PLO in its capacity as the sole legitimate representative of the Palestine people, over all liberated territory. The Arab States are pledged to uphold this authority, when it is established, in all spheres and at all levels.
3   *Supports* the PLO in the exercise of its national and international responsibilities, within the context of the principle of Arab solidarity.
4   *Invites* the Kingdom of Jordan, Syria and Egypt to formalize their relations in the light of these decisions and in order that they may be implemented.
5   *Affirms* the obligations of all Arab States to preserve Palestinian unity and not to interfere in Palestinian internal affairs.

Europa Yearbook of the Middle East and North Africa

81   Speech by Yasser Arafat, Palestine Liberation Organization, to the General Assembly, 13 November 1974

As a result of the collusion between the mandatory Power and the Zionist movement and with the support of some countries, this General Assembly early in its history approved a recommendation to partition our Palestinian homeland. This took place in an atmosphere poisoned with questionable actions and strong pressure. The General Assembly partitioned what it had no right to divide — an indivisible homeland. When we rejected that decision, our position corresponded to that of the natural mother who refused to permit King Solomon to cut her son in two when the unnatural mother claimed the child for herself and agreed to his dismemberment. Furthermore, even though the partition resolution granted the colonialist settlers 54 per cent of the land of Palestine, their dissatisfaction with the decision prompted them to wage a war of terror against the civilian Arab population. They occupied 81 per cent of the total area of Palestine, uprooting a million Arabs. Thus, they occupied 524 Arab towns and villages, of which they destroyed 385, completely obliterating them in the process. Having done so, they built their own settlements and colonies on the ruins of our farms and our groves. The roots of the Palestine question lie here. Its causes do not stem from any conflict between two religions or two nationalisms. Neither is it a border conflict between neighbouring states. It is the cause of people deprived of its homeland, dispersed and uprooted, and living mostly in exile and in refugee camps.

.   .   .

It pains our people greatly to witness the propagation of the myth that its homeland was a desert until it was made to bloom by the toil of foreign settlers, that it was a land without a people, and that the colonialist entity caused no harm to any human being. No: such lies must be exposed from this rostrum, for the world must know that Palestine was the cradle of the most ancient cultures and civilizations. Its Arab people were engaged in farming and building, spreading culture throughout the land for thousands of years, setting an example in the practice of freedom of worship, acting as faithful guardians of the holy places of all religions. As a son of Jerusalem, I treasure for myself and my people beautiful memories and vivid images of the religious brotherhood that was the hallmark of our Holy City before it succumbed (to) catastrophe. Our people continued to pursue this enlightened policy until the establishment of the State of Israel and their dispersion. This did not deter our people from pursuing their humanitarian role on Palestinian soil. Nor will they permit their land to become a launching pad for aggression or a racist camp predicated on the destruction of civilization, cultures, progress and peace. Our people cannot but maintain the heritage of their ancestors in resisting the invaders, in assuming the privileged task of defending their native land, their Arab nationhood, their culture and civilization, and in safeguarding the cradle of monotheistic religion.

.   .   .

The Palestinian people produced thousands of physicians, lawyers, teachers and scientists who actively participated in the development of the Arab countries bordering on their usurped homeland. They utilized their income to assist the young and aged amongst their people who remained in the refugee camps. They educated their younger sisters and brothers, supported their parents and cared for their children. All along, the Palestinian dreamt of return. Neither the Palestinian's allegiance to Palestine nor his determination to return waned; nothing could persuade him to relinquish his Palestinian identity or to foresake his homeland. The passage of time did not make him forget, as some hoped he would. When our people lost faith in the international community which persisted in ignoring its rights and when it became obvious that the Palestinians would not recuperate one inch of Palestine through exclusively political means, our people had no choice but to resort to armed struggle. Into that struggle it poured its material and human resources. We bravely faced the most vicious acts of Israeli terrorism which were aimed at diverting our struggle and arresting it.

In the past ten years of our struggle, thousands of martyrs and twice as many wounded, maimed and imprisoned were offered in sacrifice, all in an effort to resist the imminent threat of liquidation, to regain our right to self-determination and our undisputed right to return to our homeland. With the utmost dignity and the most admirable revolutionary spirit, our Palestinian people has not lost its spirit in Israeli prisons and concentration camps or when faced with all forms of harassment and intimidation. It struggles for sheer existence and it continues to strive to preserve the Arab character of its land. Thus it resists oppression, tyranny and terrorism in their ugliest forms.

.   .   .

The Palestine Liberation Organization has earned its legitimacy because of the sacrifice inherent in its pioneering role, and also because of its dedicated leadership of the struggle. It has also been granted this legitimacy by the Palestinian masses, which in harmony with it have chosen it to lead the struggle according to its directives. The Palestine Liberation Organization has also gained its legitimacy by representing every faction, union or group as well as every Palestinian talent, either in the National Council or in people's institutions. This legitimacy was further strengthened by the support of the entire Arab nation, and it was consecrated during the last Arab Summit Conference, which reiterated the right of the Palestine Liberation Organization, in its capacity as the sole representative of the Palestinian people, to establish an independent national State on all liberated Palestinian territory.

.   .   .

In my formal capacity as Chairman of the Palestine Liberation Organization and leader of the Palestinian revolution I proclaim before you that when we speak of our common hopes for the Palestine of tomorrow we include in our perspective all Jews now living in Palestine who choose to live with us there in peace and without discrimination.

In my formal capacity as Chairman of the Palestine Liberation Organization and leader of the Palestinian revolution I call upon Jews to turn away one by one from the illusory promises made to them by Zionist ideology and Israeli leadership. They are offering Jews perpetual bloodshed, endless war and continuous thraldom.

We invite them to emerge from their moral isolation into a more open realm of free choice, far from their present leadership's efforts to implant in them a Masada complex.

We offer them the most generous solution, that we might live together in a framework of just peace in our democratic Palestine.

In my formal capacity as Chairman of the Palestine Liberation Organization, I announce here that we do not wish one drop of either Arab or Jewish (sic) to be shed; neither do we delight in the continuation of killing, which would end once a just peace, based on our people's rights, hopes and aspirations had been finally established.

In my formal capacity as Chairman of the Palestine Liberation Organization and leader of the Palestinian revolution I appeal to you to accompany our people in its struggle to attain its right to self-determination. This right is consecrated in the United Nations Charter and has been repeatedly confirmed in resolutions adopted by this august body since the drafting of the Charter. I appeal to you, further, to aid our people's return to its homeland from an involuntary exile imposed upon it by force of arms, by tyranny, by oppression, so that we may regain our property, our land, and thereafter live in our national homeland, free and sovereign, enjoying all the privileges of nationhood. Only then can we pour all our resources into the mainstream of human civilization. Only then can Palestinian creativity be concentrated on the service of humanity. Only then will our Jerusalem resume its historic role as a peaceful shrine for all religions.

I appeal to you to enable our people to establish national independent sovereignty over its own land.

Today I have come bearing an olive branch and a freedom-fighter's gun. Do not let the olive branch fall from my hand. I repeat: do not let the olive branch fall from my hand.

War flares up in Palestine, and yet it is in Palestine that peace will be born.

UNO, GAOR, 29th Session, Two
Thousand Two Hundred and Eighty-
Second Meeting, A/PV. 2282/Corr. 1

82   Speech by Yosef Tekoah, Israel, to the General Assembly, 13 November 1974

On 14 October 1974 the General Assembly turned its back on the
UN Charter, on law and humanity, and virtually capitulated to a
murder organization which aims at the destruction of a State Member
of the UN. On 14 October the UN hung out a sign reading
'Murderers of children are welcome here.'

Today these murderers have come to the General Assembly, certain
that it would do their bidding. Today this rostrum was defiled by their
chieftain, who proclaimed that the shedding of Jewish blood would
end only when the murderers' demands had been accepted and their
objectives achieved.

On 14 October the UN and Governments which made the invitation
to the Palestine Liberation Organization (PLO) possible became the
object of worldwide criticism. Editorials and caricatures in the press
and demonstrations on all continents expressed revulsion at the
spectacle of the UN tearing asunder its own principles and precepts
and paying homage to bloodshed and bestiality.

Today bloodshed and bestiality have come here to collect the spoils
of the UN surrender. This surrender must be absolute they told the
world this morning. The victim of bloodshed and bestiality should not
even defend himself.

The United Nations is entrusted with the responsibility to guide
mankind away from war, away from violence and oppression, toward
peace, toward international understanding and the vindication of the
rights of peoples and individuals. What remains of that responsibility
now that the UN has prostrated itself before the PLO, which stands for
premeditated, deliberate murder of innocent civilians, denies to the
Jewish people its right to live, and seeks to destroy the Jewish State by
armed force?

.   .   .

Are the Arabs of Palestine suffering starvation as are, according to
UN statistics, almost 500 million people in Asia, Africa and Latin
America? Has the UN left the Palestinian refugees without assistance
as it has tens of millions of refugees all over the world, including Jewish

refugees in Israel from Arab lands? Are the Palestinian refugees the only ones who cannot be reintegrated as others have been? Have the Palestinian Arabs no State of their own? What is Jordan if not a Palestinian Arab State?

The real reason for the special consideration accorded to questions concerning the Arabs of Palestine has been one and one only—the continuous exploitation of these questions as a weapon of Arab belligerency against Israel. As King Hussein said of the Arab leaders: 'They have used the Palestine people for selfish political purposes.' This is also the real motivation of the present debate,

In fact, no nation has enjoyed greater fulfilment of its political rights, no nation has been endowed with territory, sovereignty and independence more abundantly than the Arabs.

Now, as a result of centuries of acquisition of territory by war, the Arab nation is represented in the UN by twenty sovereign States. Among them is also the Palestinian Arab State of Jordan.

Geographically and ethnically Jordan is Palestine. Historically both the West and East Banks of the Jordan river are parts of the Land of Israel or Palestine. Both were parts of Palestine under the British Mandate until Jordan and then Israel became independent. The population of Jordan is composed of two elements—the sedentary population and nomads. Both are, of course, Palestinian. The nomad Bedouins constitute a minority of Jordan's population. Moreover, the majority of the sedentary inhabitants, even on the East Bank, are of Palestinian West Bank origin. Without the Palestinians, Jordan is a State without a people.

That is why when on 29 April 1950 King Abdullah inaugurated the commemorative session of the Jordanian Parliament he declared: 'I open the session of the Parliament with both banks of the Jordan united by the will of the people, one homeland and one hope.'

On 23 August 1959, the Prime Minister of Jordan stated: 'We are the Government of Palestine, the army of Palestine and the refugees of Palestine.'

Indeed, the vast majority of Palestinian refugees never left Palestine, but moved, as a result of the 1948 and 1967 wars, from one part of the country to another. At the same time, an approximately equal number of Jewish refugees fled from Arab countries to Israel.

It is, therefore, false to allege that the Palestinian people has been deprived of a State of its own or that it has been uprooted from its national homeland. Most Palestinians continue to live in Palestine.

Most Palestinians continue to live in a Palestinian State. The vast majority of Palestinian Arabs are citizens of that Palestinian State.

.   .   .

The choice before the General Assembly is clear. On the one hand there is the Charter of the UN; on the other there is the PLO, whose sinister objectives, defined in its Covenant, and savage outrages are a desecration of the Charter.

On the one hand, there is Israel's readiness and desire to reach a peaceful settlement with the Palestinian Arab State of Jordan in which the Palestinian national identity would find full expression. On the other hand there is the PLO's denial of Israel's right to independence and of the Jewish people's right to self-determination.

The choice is between understanding and continued conflict in the Middle East, between suppression of terror and its encouragement, between satisfying the needs of the Palestinians through the peace-making process already under way or undermining that process by trying to introduce into it a murder organization which aims at the elimination of one of the negotiating states.

The question is: should there be peace between Israel and its eastern neighbour or should an attempt be made to establish a Palestine Liberation Organization base to the east of Israel from which the terrorist campaign against the Jewish State's existence could be pursued?

On 14 October the General Assembly opted for the PLO, it opted for terrorism, it opted for savagery. Can there be any hope that it might now undo the harm it has already done, by that action, to the cause of peace in the Middle East and to humanity in general? Israel has also made its choice.

The United Nations, whose duty it is to combat terrorism and barbarity may agree to consort with them. Israel will not.

The murderers of athletes in the Olympic Games of Munich, the butchers of children in Ma'alot, the assassins of diplomats in Khartoum do not belong in the international community. They have no place in international diplomatic efforts. Israel shall see to it that they have no place in them.

Israel will pursue the PLO murderers until justice is meted out to them. It will continue to take action against their organization and against their bases until a definitive end is put to their atrocities. The blood of Jewish children will not be shed with impunity.

Israel will not permit the establishment of PLO authority in any part of Palestine. The PLO will not be forced on the Palestinian Arabs. It will not be tolerated by the Jews of Israel.

UNO, GAOR, 29th Session, Two Thousand Two Hundred and Eighty-Second Meeting, A/PV. 2283

83   General Assembly Resolution 3236(XXIX), 22 November 1974

The General Assembly
Having considered the question of Palestine,
Having heard the statement of the Palestine Liberation Organization, the representative of the Palestinian people,
Having also heard other statements made during the debate,
Deeply concerned that no just solution to the problem of Palestine has yet been achieved and recognizing that the problem of Palestine continues to endanger international peace and security,
Recognizing that the Palestinian people is entitled to self-determination in accordance with the Charter of the United Nations,
Expressing its grave concern that the Palestinian people has been prevented from enjoying its inalienable rights, in particular its right to self-determination,
Guided by the purposes and principles of the Charter,
Recalling its relevant resolutions which affirm the right of the Palestinian people to self-determination,
1   *Reaffirms* the inalienable rights of the Palestinian people in Palestine, including:
(a) The right of self-determination without external interference;
(b) The right to national independence and sovereignty;
2   *Reaffirms also* the inalienable right of the Palestinians to return to their homes and property from which they have been displaced and uprooted, and calls for their return;
3   *Emphasizes* that full respect for and the realization of these inalienable rights of the Palestinian people are indispensable for the solution of the question of Palestine;
4   *Recognizes* that the Palestinian people is a principal party in the establishment of a just and durable peace in the Middle East;
5   *Further recognizes* the right of the Palestinian people to regain its rights by all means in accordance with the purposes and principles of the Charter of the United Nations;

6   *Appeals* to all States and international organizations to extend their support to the Palestinian people in its struggle to restore its rights, in accordance with the Charter;
7   *Requests* the Secretary-General to establish contacts with the Palestine Liberation Organization on all matters concerning with question of Palestine;
8   *Requests* the Secretary-General to report to the General Assembly at its thirtieth session on the implementation of the present resolution;
9   *Decides* to include the item 'Question of Palestine' in the provisional agenda of its thirtieth session.

UNO, doc. BR/74/55(1974)

84   The Sinai Agreement, initialed in Jerusalem and Alexandria, 1 September 1975, and signed at Geneva, 4 September 1975

AGREEMENT BETWEEN EGYPT AND ISRAEL.

The Government of the Arab Republic of Egypt and the Government of Israel have agreed that:

ARTICLE I

The conflict between them in the Middle East shall not be resolved by military force but by peaceful means.

The Agreement concluded by the Parties 18 January 1974, within the framework of the Geneva Peace Conference, constituted a first step towards a just and durable peace according to the provisions of Security Council Resolution 338 of 22 October 1973.

They are determined to reach a final and just peace settlement by means of negotiations called for by Security Council Resolution 338, this Agreement being a significant step towards that end.

ARTICLE II

The Parties hereby undertake not to resort to the threat or use of force or military blockade against each other.

ARTICLE III

The Parties shall continue scrupulously to observe the ceasefire on land, sea and air and to refrain from all military or para-military actions against each other.

The Parties also confirm that the obligations contained in the Annex and, when concluded, the Protocol shall be an integral part of this Agreement.

ARTICLE IV

A   The military forces of the Parties shall be deployed in accordance with the following principles:[1]

1   All Israeli forces shall be deployed east of the lines designated as Lines J and M on the attached map.

2   All Egyptian forces shall be deployed west of the line designated as Line E on the attached map.

3   The area between the lines designated on the attached map as Lines E and F and the area between the lines designated on the attached map as Lines J and K shall be limited in armament and forces.

4   The limitations on armament and forces in the areas described by paragraph (3) above shall be agreed as described in the attached annex.

5   The zone between the lines designated on the attached map as Lines E and J, will be a buffer zone. In this zone, the United Nations Emergency Force will continue to perform its functions as under the Egyptian-Israeli Agreement of 18 January 1974.

6   In the area south from Line E and west from Line M, as defined on the attached map, there will be no military forces, as specified in the attached Annex.

B   The details concerning the new lines, the redeployment of the forces and its timing, the limitation on armaments and forces, aerial reconnaissance, the operation of the early warning and surveillance installations and the use of the roads, the United Nations functions and under other arrangements will all be in accordance with the provisions of the Annex and map which are an integral part of this Agreement and of the Protocol which is to result from negotiations pursuant to the Annex and which, when concluded, shall become an integral part of this Agreement.

ARTICLE V

The United Nations Emergency Force is essential and shall continue its functions and its mandate shall be extended annually.

ARTICLE VI

The Parties hereby establish a Joint Commission for the duration of this Agreement. It will function under the aegis of the Chief Coordinator of the United Nations Peacekeeping Missions in the Middle East in order to consider any problem arising from this Agreement and to assist the United Nations Emergency Force in the

1   See Map 3.

execution of its mandate. The Joint Commission shall function in accordance with procedures established in the Protocol.

ARTICLE VII

Non-military cargoes destined for or coming from Israel shall be permitted through the Suez Canal.

ARTICLE VIII

This Agreement is regarded by the Parties as a significant step towards a just and lasting peace. It is not a final agreement.

The Parties shall continue their efforts to negotiate a final peace agreement within the framework of the Geneva Peace Conference in accordance with Security Council Resolution 338

ARTICLE IX

This Agreement shall enter into force upon signature of the Protocol and remain in force until superseded by a new agreement.

> Department of State. Selected Documents No. 4. US Policy in the Middle East: November 1974-February 1976

85 Statement by Secretary of State Henry Kissinger before the Senate Committee on Foreign Relations, 7 October 1975

I welcome this opportunity to appear before your committee to testify on the recent agreement between Israel and Egypt. That agreement — if carried out in good faith by both parties — may well mark a historic turning point, away from the cycle of war and stalemate that has for so long afflicted Israelis and Arabs and the world at large. I am here to urge prompt and positive congressional action to help further the prospects for peace in the Middle East.

For more than 30 years the issues in that troubled region have been recognized by successive American Administrations as having profound consequences for America's own interests. The US diplomatic role in the Middle East is a matter of vital national importance.

— We have a historic and moral commitment to the survival and security of Israel.

— We have important interests in the Arab world with its 150 million people and the world's largest oil reserves.

— We know that the world's hopes and our own, for economic recovery and progress could be dashed by another upheaval in the Middle East.

— We must avoid the severe strains on our relations with our allies in

Europe and Japan that perpetual crises in the Middle East would almost certainly entail.

– We face the dangers of a direct US-Soviet confrontation, with its attendant nuclear risk, if tension in the Middle East should increase.

The October war of 1973 brought home to every American, in concrete and dramatic ways, the price we pay for continued Arab-Israeli conflict. The oil embargo triggered by that war cost us 500,000 jobs, more than $10 billion in national production, and a rampant inflation. The 1973 crisis put our alliances with Western Europe and Japan under the most severe strain they had ever known. And it brought us to the verge of a confrontation with the Soviet Union, requiring us to place our military forces on a global alert.

Thus for the most basic reasons of national policy we owe it to the American people to do all we can to insure that the Middle East moves toward peace and away from conflict.

.   .   .

It is our strong conviction that the Sinai agreement is indispensable to the process of peace. Were I here today to report that we had failed to obtain a Sinai agreement, I would have to tell you as well that the prospects of still another Arab-Israeli war were infinitely and eminently greater. Instead, I can state that the prospects for peace in the Middle East have been significantly advanced and that good chances exist for even further progress – if we have the wisdom and national will to seize the opportunity before us.

Hailed by both Prime Minister Rabin and President Sadat as a possible turning point, the Sinai agreement represents the most far-reaching, practical test of peace – political, military, and psychological – in the long and tragic history of the Arab-Israeli conflict. For the first time in more than two decades, Israel and an Arab state have agreed not just to disentangle their forces in the aftermath of war but to commit themselves to the peaceful resolution of the differences that for so long have made them mortal enemies.

Department of State. Selected Documents No. 4. US Policy in the Middle East: November 1974-February 1976

X

The Egyptian-Israeli Peace Treaty

Frustrated by the lack of progress at Geneva and believing that the new right-wing coalition government of Menachem Begin, which had emerged victorious from the May 1977 elections, was strong enough to be able to make concessions, President Sadat initiated diplomatic moves which may fairly be said to have set Middle Eastern affairs on a new course. The first public indication that he was prepared to put the Arab case before the Knesset came on 9 November 1977 (**86**), an offer which Israel accepted the following day. His speech at the historic Knesset meeting on 20 November is given in full in document **87**, followed by Prime Minister Begin's response (**88**).

Despite the initial euphoria generated by President Sadat's visit to Jerusalem, detailed negotiations between the two countries stalled badly, with Egypt, conscious of the disapproval felt elsewhere in the Arab world, working for a comprehensive Middle Eastern settlement, and Israel holding out in the hope of achieving a bilateral treaty. Once again, American diplomatic intervention proved necessary (**89**) with President Carter convening a summit meeting at Camp David from 5 to 17 September 1978. Documents **90** and **91** constitute the principal agreements reached, the 'Framework for the Conclusion of a Peace Between Egypt and Israel', and the 'Framework for Peace in the Middle East agreed at Camp David'. The latter established that there would be negotiations over the future of the Palestinians of the West Bank and Gaza, but begged a number of questions, not least being the failure to define 'autonomy'. The Camp David agreements were condemned by the Arab states of the 'Steadfastness Front' at a meeting in Damascus (**92**).

As differences between Egypt and Israel continued to plague their negotiations for a peace treaty, American mediation proved necessary when the three months envisaged in the Camp David 'Framework' lapsed without agreement on a text. After intensive diplomacy by President Carter, Secretary of State Cyrus Vance and their officials, the 'Treaty of Peace between the Arab Republic of Egypt and the State of Israel' (**93**) was signed at Washington on 26 March 1979. It had been achieved at considerable cost to Egypt's relations with the other Arab states and difficult negotiations lay ahead over Gaza and the West Bank, where ultra-religious Israeli settlers were trying to establish themselves; but its significance for the Middle East was undeniable.

86   President Sadat's speech to the People's Assembly, 9 November 1977

My call for peace preceded the war, accompanied it, and then followed it. On 4 February 1971, from this rostrum, I took the initiative and called upon Israel to carry out a partial withdrawal on the eastern bank of the Canal as a first phase in a timetable that would be worked out later to implement the remaining provisions of Resolution 242. I said that in return, we would be prepared to clear the Suez Canal and reopen it to international shipping to serve the world economy.

At the peak of our immortal military victory, from this rostrum on 16 October 1973, I once again announced to the world an initiative calling for the convening of an international peace conference under the auspices of the United Nations with the participation of the representatives of the heroic Palestinian people in their capacity as an essential party to the issue.

That initiative was in fact the first spark which produced the Geneva conference. It was then that Israel, for the first time since its establishment, found itself with an option which it could not escape from or tamper with — nor could it continue to deceive public opinion by claiming that it desired peace while the Arabs rejected it.

.   .   .

In September 1975 when we were negotiating the second disengagement, Henry Kissinger used to travel from Tel Aviv to Alexandria, where I was at the time, to meet me to change a word, a vowel, a letter or a sentence. On one occasion I said to him: This is an odd business. This effort is not worth the fuel which you are consuming to come from Tel Aviv to Alexandria. But this is the character of the Israelis.

You have just heard me say that we are not conerned at all about procedural matters. I tell you frankly, our people and the entire world: We are prepared to go to Geneva and sit there for the sake of peace, irrespective of all the procedural claims Israel is making in its desire to make us lose the opportunity or to make us nervous so that we may say, as we have said in the past that no, we do not want to go and we will not go and then Israel will appear to the world as the advocate of peace. Never. I agree to any procedural process. Why? Because when we eventually go to Geneva, Israel will not be able to prevent me from demanding the return of the Arab territory occupied in 1967. Neither Israel nor any power will be able to stop the demand for the legitimate rights—the right to self-determination and the right of the Palestinians to establish their state.

That is what Israel wants to avoid by trying to play with the procedural process by adding a word or omitting a word or by issuing a declaration after an Israeli Cabinet meeting by which they try to excite the Arab nation as they used to do in the past in order that we may have a nervous breakdown, that some may suffer a fit and that we may come out and say: We do not want to go to Geneva. No, never. I declare before you and the Arab nation that I am not interested at all in procedural processes. Let there be procedures. Regardless of Israel's emotionalism and hysteria, I am going to Geneva. As I have said, neither Israel nor the world powers can dissuade me from what I want—the Arab territory occupied in 1967 and the rights of the Palestinian people, including their right to establish their state.

As long as this is my conviction, it is Israel which fears the Geneva conference. No Arab must ever fear the Geneva conference. Why? It is because we have exported to the Israeli society the division, fear, defeatism, doubt and suspicion and everything that we suffered from in the past.

Why should we return to that state? No, never. I am ready to go to Geneva. I will not hide it from you as representatives of the people and I say it for all our people here and for our Arab nation to hear—and you have heard me say it—I am ready to go to the ends of the earth if this will prevent a soldier or an officer of my sons from being wounded—not being killed, but wounded.

I say now that I am ready to go to the ends of the earth. Israel will be astonished when it hears me saying now before you that I am ready to go to their house, to the Knesset itself, and to talk to them.

SWB, ME/5664/A3 – 13

87   President Sadat's address to the Knesset, 20 November 1977

In the Name of God, Mr Speaker of the Knesset, ladies and gentlemen, permit me first to address a special thanks to the Speaker of the Knesset for giving me this opportunity to address you.

I begin my speech by saying God's peace and mercy be with you. God willing, peace for us all. Peace for us in the Arab land and in Israel and in every part of the land of this wide world, this world which is made complex by its bloody conflicts and which is made tense by its sharp contradictions and which is threatened every now and then by destructive wars — wars made by man to kill his brother man and, in the end, amid the debris and mutilated bodies of men, there is neither victor nor vanquished. The true vanquished one is always man, man which is the best of God's creation, man which God created, as Gandhi the saint of peace has stated, to walk on his feet to build life and worship God.

Today, I come to you with both feet firmly on the ground, in order that we may build a new life and so that we may establish peace. All of us in this land, the land of God, Moslems, Christians and Jews, worship God and no other god. God's decrees and commandments are: love, honesty, chastity and peace.

I can excuse all those who received my decision to attend your assembly, when I made that decision known to the whole world — I can say I can excuse all those who received my decision with astonishment, or rather who were flabbergasted. Some, under the effect of this violent surprise, thought that my decision was nothing more than a verbal manoeuvre, for home consumption and before world opinion; others described it as a political tactic to conceal my intentions to wage a fresh war.

I do not want to conceal from you that one of my aides at the Presidency Office contacted me, at a late hour after I returned home from the People's Assembly, to ask me, with concern: What are you going to do if Israel actually addresses an invitation to you? I replied quite calmly: I shall immediately accept it. I have declared that I am ready to go to the end of the world; I shall go to Israel, because I want to put before the people of Israel the full facts.

I can excuse anyone who was flabbergasted by the decision or who had doubts about the sound intentions behind that declaration. No one could imagine that the President of the largest Arab State, which bears the greatest burden and first responsibility over the question of war or peace in the Middle East region, could take a decision to be prepared to go to enemy territory when we are in a state of war, and we and you are still suffering the effects of four severe wars in a period of 30 years. All this, at the time when the families of the war of October 1973 are still living out the tragedies of losing husbands and sons and the martyrdom of fathers and sisters.

However, as I have already declared, I did not discuss this decision with any of my colleagues and brother heads of the Arab states, not even those of the confrontation states; some of them who got in touch with me after the announcement opposed the decision, because a state of total doubt still existed in everybody's mind, a state of complete lack of confidence between the Arab states, including the Palestinian people, and Israel.

Suffice it to say that long months during which peace could have been established have been wasted in useless differences and discussions over procedures concerning the convening of the Geneva conference; all of them reflected this total doubt, this total lack of confidence. But, I tell you frankly and with complete sincerity that I took this decision after long thought; and I know quite well that it is a big gamble. But if Almighty God has made it my destiny to assume responsibility for the people of Egypt, and to have a share in the responsibility for the destiny of the entire Arab people, then I think that the first duty dictated by this responsibility is that I must exhaust every possibility in order to stop the Arab people of Egypt, and all the Arab peoples, from enduring the sufferings of other horrendous, destructive wars — only God knows their extent.

After long thought, I was convinced that my responsibility to God and the people imposes on me the obligation to go to the furthest place in the world and, indeed, to come to Jerusalem to speak to the members of the Knesset, the representatives of the people of Israel, about all the facts which I have in my own mind. Afterwards, I shall let you to decide by yourselves and let Almighty God do whatever he wishes with us after that.

Ladies and gentlemen: There are moments in the life of nations and peoples when those who are known for their wisdom and foresight are required to look beyond the past, with all its complications and remnants, for the sake of a courageous upsurge towards new horizons. These people who, like ourselves, shoulder that responsibility entrusted to us are the first people who must have the courage to take fateful decisions in harmony with the sublimity of the situation.

We must rise above all forms of fanaticism and self-deception and obsolete theories of superiority. It is important that we should never forget that virtue is God's alone. If I say that I want to protect the Arab people from the terrors of new, terrifying wars, I declare before you with all sincerity that I have the same feelings and I carry the same responsibility for every human being in the world and, most certainly, for the Israeli people.

A life which is taken away in war is the life of a human being, whether it is an Arab or an Israeli life. The wife who becomes a widow is a human being and has the right to live in a happy family environment whether she is an Arab or an Israeli. The innocent children who lose the care and love of their parents are all our children; they are all our children, whether in the land of the Arabs or in Israel; we have a great responsibility to provide them with a prosperous present and a better future. For all these reasons and to protect the life of all our sons and sisters and in order that our communities may produce in safety and security for the development and happiness of man and give him the right to a dignified life, and out of responsibility to the future generations, in order to achieve a smile on the face of every child born in our land — for all these reasons I have taken my decision to come to you to speak directly to you.

I have borne, and shall continue to bear the requirements of a historic responsibility. For this reason some years ago — to be precise on 4 February 1971 — I declared that I was ready to sign a peace agreement with Israel. This was the first declaration to come from a responsible Arab since the beginning of the Arab-Israeli conflict.

With all these motives, which are made necessary by the responsibility of leadership, I declared on 16 October 1973 and before the Egyptian People's Assembly that an international conference should be called to determine a lasting and just peace. I was not then in a position to beg for peace or seek a cease-fire. With all these motives, which are made imperative by the duty of history and leadership, we signed the first disengagement agreement and then the second one, on Sinai. Then we tried to knock on open and closed doors to find a specific road towards a lasting and just peace. We have opened our hearts to all the peoples of the world so that they may understand our motives and aims and so that they may really be convinced that we are advocates of justice and seekers of peace.

For all these reasons too, I decided to come to you with an open mind and an open heart and a conscientious will so that we may establish a lasting and just peace.

Destiny has decreed that my visit to you, my visit of peace, should come on the day of the great Islamic feast, the blessed Id al-Adha, the feast of sacrifice and redemption when Ibrahim [Abraham], may peace be upon him, the forefather of both the Arabs and the Jews, our father Ibrahim submitted to God and dedicated himself completely to Him, not through weakness but through colossal spiritual power and through his free choice to sacrifice his son, which arose from his firm, unshakable belief in the sublime ideals which gave a deep meaning to life.

Perhaps this coincidence has a new meaning for us all; perhaps it forms a concrete hope for the good signs of security and safety and peace.

Ladies and gentlemen, let us be frank with each other, using straightforward words and clear thoughts which cannot be twisted. Let us be frank with each other today when the whole world, East and West, is following this unique event, this event which could be a turning-point, which could mean a radical change in the history of this part of the world, if not in the whole world. Let us be frank with each other; let us be frank with each other when answering the big question: How can we achieve a just and lasting peace?

First of all, I have come to you bringing with me a clear and frank answer to this major question, so that the people of Israel can hear it; the whole world can hear it; all those whose sincere calls reach me can hear it; and so that the results hoped for by millions of people may materialize from this historic meeting.

Before I make my answer known to you, I want to stress that in this clear and frank answer I rely on a number of facts, facts which no-one can deny. The first fact is that there can be no happiness for some (people) at the expense of the misery of others. The second fact is that I have not spoken and will not speak in two tongues, nor have I used nor shall I use two policies; I deal with everyone with one tongue, one policy and one face. The third fact is that direct confrontation and a straight line are the nearest and most useful methods to achieve the clear aim. The fourth fact is that the call for a just and lasting peace based on the implementation of the UN resolutions has today become the call of all the world, and has become a clear expression of the will of the international community, both at the level of the official capitals—where policy is decided and decisions made—and at the level of world opinion, which influences the policy and decisions.

The fifth fact—and perhaps it is the most obvious one—is that, in its efforts to achieve a just and lasting peace, the Arab nation is not proceeding from a position of weakness or (? instability); quite the contrary: Its strength and stability are such that its efforts must stem from a genuine desire for peace, from a realization that for the spirit of civilization to survive, for us, you and the whole world to avoid a real disaster, there is no alternative to the establishment of a lasting and just peace that no storms can shake, no doubts can spoil, and no ill-intentions can undermine.

On the basis of these facts — these facts that I wanted to convey to you as I see them — I would like with complete sincerity to warn you about certain thoughts that might cross your minds; the duty to be sincere means that I must state the following:

Firstly, I did not come to you with a view to concluding a separate agreement between Egypt and Israel, this is not provided for in Egypt's policy. The problem does not lie just between Egypt and Israel; moreover, no separate peace between Egypt and Israel — or between any confrontation state and Israel — could secure a lasting and just peace in the region as a whole. Even if a peace agreement was achieved between all the confrontation states and Israel, without a just solution to the Palestinian problem it would never ensure the establishment of the durable, lasting peace the entire world is now trying to achieve.

Secondly, I did not come with a view of securing a partial peace, a peace such that we end the state of war at this stage, and then postpone the whole problem to a second phase. This is not the fundamental solution that will lead us to a lasting peace. Linked to this is the fact that I did not come to you in order that we may agree to a third disengagement of forces either in Sinai alone, or in Sinai, the Golan and the West Bank; this would be merely a postponement of an explosion until a later time. It would also mean that we lacked the courage to face up to peace, we were too weak to shoulder the burden and responsibilities of a lasting and just peace.

I have come to you so that together we can build a lasting and just peace, so that not one more drop of the blood of either side may be shed. For this reason I stated that I was willing to go to the ends of the earth. At this point I shall answer the question: How are we going to achieve permanent and just peace? In my opinion, and I say it from this platform to the whole world, to find an answer is not impossible and neither it is difficult, despite the long years of blood revenge, hatred and rancour, of bringing up generations on terms of complete estrangement and entrenched enmity. The answer is not difficult nor impossible to find, if we follow the path of a straight line with all honesty and faith. You want to live with us in this area of the world, and I say to you with all sincerity that we welcome you among us with security and safety.

This in itself forms a giant turning-point, a decisive landmark of an historic transformation. We used to reject you, and we had our reasons and grievances. Yes, we used to reject meeting you anywhere. Yes, we used to describe you as 'so-called Israel'. Yes, conferences and international organizations used to bring us together. Our representatives have never and still do not exchange greetings and salaams. Yes, this is what happened, and it still goes on. For any talks, we used (to) make it conditional that a mediator met each side separately. Yes, this is how the talks on the first disengagement were conducted and this is also how the talks on the second disengagement were held. Our representatives met at the first Geneva conference without exchanging one direct word. Yes, this is what went on. But I say to you today and I say to the whole world that we accept that we should live with you in a lasting and just peace. We do not want to surround you or to be surrounded ourselves with missiles which are ready to destroy, with the missiles of hatred and bitterness.

More than once, I have said that Israel has become a living reality. The world recognized it and the two superpowers shouldered the responsibility of its security and the defence of its existence. And when we want peace both in theory and in practice we welcome you to live amongst us in security and peace, in theory and practice.

There existed between you and us a huge high wall. You tried to build it over quarter of a century, but it was demolished in 1973. In its ferocity the wall continued the war psychologically. Your wall was a threat with a force capable of destroying the Arab nation from end to end. The wall was based on the view that the Arab peoples had turned into a nation with no defences. Indeed some of you said that even after another 50 years the Arabs would never achieve a position of any strength.

This wall has always threatened, with a long arm capable of reaching any position over any distance. This wall has threatened us with annihilation and extinction if we tried to exercise our legitimate right of liberating the occupied territory.

We must admit together that this wall has fallen, it collapsed in 1973. But there is still another wall, this second wall forms a complex psychological barrier between us and you. It is a barrier of doubt, a barrier of hatred, a barrier of fear of deception, a barrier of illusions about behaviour, actions or decisions, a barrier of cautious and mistaken interpretation of every event or statement. This psychological barrier is the one I have mentioned in official statements, which in my opinion constitutes 70 per cent of the problem.

On my visit to you, I ask you today why we do not extend our hands in sincerity, faith and truth so that we may together destroy this barrier? Why we do not make our intentions the same in truth, faith and sincerity so that we may together eliminate all the doubt, the fear of treachery and ill-intentions, and prove the sincerity of our intentions. Why do we not join together, with the courage of men and the daring of heroes of those who risk their lives for the sake of a sublime ideal? Why do we not join together with this courage and daring to set up a mammoth edifice of peace, an edifice that builds and does not destroy, that emits to our future generations the light of the human spirit for building, development and the good of man? Why should we leave for these generations the consequences of the bloodletting, the killing of souls, the orphaning of children, the making of widows, the destruction of families and the agony of victims?

Why do we not believe in the wisdom of the Creator, as conveyed in the Proverbs of the wise Solomon: Deceit is in the heart of those who imagine evil, but to the advocates of peace will come joy; better a morsel and peace than a house full of meat with strife. Why don't we repeat together, why don't we sing together from the psalms of David: Hear the voice of my supplications when I cry unto Thee, when I lift up my hands towards Thy holy oracle. Put me not with the wicked and with the evil-doers, who speak of peace to their neighbours, but have evil in their hearts. Treat them according to their actions, according to the wickedness of their deeds. I ask for peace and seek it.

Ladies and gentlemen, the truth is — and it is the truth that I am telling you — that there can be no peace in the true sense of the word, unless this peace is based on justice and not on the occupation of the territory of others. It is not right that you seek for yourselves what you deny to others. In all frankness and in the spirit which prompted me to come to you, I say to you: you have finally to abandon the dreams of tomorrow and you have also to abandon the belief that force is the best means of dealing with the Arabs. You have to absorb very well the lessons of confrontation between ourselves and you; expansion will be of no avail to you.

To put it clearly, our territory is not a subject of bargaining; it is not a topic for wrangling. To us, the national and nationalist soil occupies the same position which the sacred valley of Tuwa occupies — the valley in which God spoke to Moses, may the peace of God be on him. None of us has the right to accept or to forfeit one inch of it, or to accept the principle of bargaining and wrangling about it. The truth is — and it is the truth that I am telling you — that before us today is a favourable opportunity for peace; it is an opportunity the like of which time will not provide again, if we are really serious in the struggle for peace. It is an opportunity which, if we miss it or waste it, the curse of mankind and of history will be on those who plotted against it.

What is peace to Israel? To live in the region, together with her Arab neighbours, in security and safety—this is a logic to which I say: 'Yes'. For Israel to live within her borders secure from any aggression—this is a logic to which I say: 'Yes'. For Israel to get all kinds of assurances that ensure for her these two facts—this is a demand to which I say: 'Yes'.

Furthermore, we declare that we accept all the international assurances which you can imagine and from those whom you approve. We declare that we accept all assurances you want from the two superpowers; or from one of them; or from the big five; or from some of them. I repeat and I declare quite clearly that we accept any guarantees you need because in return we shall take the same guarantees.

The upshot of the matter then is this—when we put the question: What is peace to Israel? The answer would be: That it lives within its borders together with its Arab neighbours in security and safety and within the framework of all that it likes in the way of guarantees which the other side obtains. But how can this be achieved? How can we arrive at this result so that it can take us to a permanent and just peace?

There are facts that must be confronted with all courage and clarity. There is Arab land which Israel has occupied and still occupies by armed force. And we insist that complete withdrawal from this land be undertaken and this includes Arab Jerusalem, Jerusalem to which I have come, as it is considered the city of peace and which has been and will always be the living embodiment of coexistence between believers of the three religions. It is inadmissible for anyone to think of Jerusalem's special position within the context of annexation and expansion. It must be made a free city, open to all the faithful. What is more important is that the city must not be closed to those who have chosen it as a place of residence for several centuries.

Instead of inflaming the feuds of the wars of the crusades we must revive the spirit of Umar Bin al-Khattab and Saladin, that is the spirit of tolerance and respect for rights. The Moslem and Christian houses of worship are not mere places for the performance of religious rites and prayers. They are the true testimonies of our uninterrupted existence in this place, politically, morally and ideologically. Here, nobody must miscalculate the importance and veneration we hold for Jerusalem, we Christians and Moslems.

Let me tell you without hesitation that I have not come to you, under this dome, to beg you to withdraw your forces from the occupied territory. This is because complete withdrawal from the Arab territories occupied after 1967 is a matter that goes without saying, over which we accept no controversy and in respect of which there is no begging to anyone or from anyone. There will be no meaning to talk about a lasting, just peace and there will be no meaning to any step to guarantee our lives together in this part of the world in peace and security while you occupy an Arab land by armed forces. There can never be peace established or built with the occupation of other's land. Yes, this is a self-evident truth, which accepts no controversy or discussion once the intentions are true — once the intentions are true, as is the struggle for the establishment of a lasting, just peace for our generation and for all the generations that will follow us.

As regards the Palestine question, nobody denies that it is the essence of the entire problem. Nobody throughout the entire world accepts today slogans raised here in Israel which disregard the existence of the people of Palestine and even ask where the people of Palestine are. The problem of the Palestinian people, and the legitimate rights of the Palestinian people are now no longer ignored or rejected by anybody; no thinking mind supposes that they could be ignored or rejected; they are facts that meet with the support and recognition of the international community both in the West and the East and in international documents and official declarations. No one could turn a deaf ear to their loud, resounding sound, or turn a blind eye to their historic reality.

Even the USA — your first ally, which is the most committed to the protection of the existence and security of Israel and which has been giving Israel and continues to give it moral, material and military aid — I say even the USA has opted for facing up to the reality and to facts, to recognize that the Palestinian people have legitimate rights, and that the Palestine question is the crux and essence of the conflict; and that so long as this question remains suspended without a solution the conflict will increase, grow more intense and reach new magnitudes.

In all sincerity, I tell you that peace cannot be achieved without the Palestinians, and that it would be a great mistake, the effect of which no one knows, to turn a blind eye to this question or to set it aside.

I shall not recall events of the past, since the issue of the Balfour Declaration 60 years ago. You know the facts quite well. And if you have found it legally and morally justified to set up a national homeland on a land that was not totally yours, you are well placed to show understanding to the insistence of the Palestinian people to set up their own state anew, on their homeland.

When some hard-liners and extremists demand that the Palestinians should abandon this higher aim it means, in reality and in actual fact, that this is a demand that they should abandon their identity and every hope they have for the future. I salute some Israeli voices which demanded that the rights of the Palestinian people should be recognized in order to achieve and guarantee peace. Therefore, Ladies and Gentlemen, I say to you that there is no benefit from not recognizing the Palestinian people and their rights to establish their state and to return home. We, the Arabs, have earlier experienced this, over you and the truth of the existence of Israel. The struggle took us from one war to another and from victims to more victims, until we and you have reached today the brink of a terrifying abyss and a frigthening disaster if, today, we do not seize together the chance of a permanent and just peace.

You must face the reality courageously, as I have faced it. It is no solution to a problem to run away from it or to be above it. There can never be peace through an attempt to impose imaginary situations on which the entire world has turned its back and declared its unanimous appeal that right and justice should be respected. There is no need to enter the vicious circle of Palestinian rights. There is no use in creating obstacles, for either they will delay the march of peace or peace itself will be killed.

As I have already told you, there can be no happiness for some at the expense of the misery of others; direct confrontation and the straight line are the surest and most useful ways of reaching the clear aim. Direct confrontation of the Palestine problem and the only language to tackle it to reach a just and lasting peace are in establishing their state, with all the international reassurances you want. You must have no fear of a young state which needs the assistance of all the states in the world to establish itself.

When the bells of peace ring, there will be no hand to beat the drums of war; should such a hand exist, it will not be heard. Imagine with me the peace agreement in Geneva, the good news of which we herald to a world thirsty for peace: (Firstly) a peace agreement based on ending the Israeli occupation of the Arab territory occupied in 1967; (secondly) the realization of basic rights of the Palestinian people and this people's right to self-determination, including their right to setting up their own state; thirdly, the right of all the countries of the region to live in peace within their secure and guaranteed borders, through agreed measures for the appropriate security of international borders, in addition to the appropriate international guarantees; fourthly, all the States in the region will undertake to administer relations among themselves in accordance with the principles and aims of the UN Charter, in particular eschewing the use of force and settling differences among them by peaceful means; and fifthly, ending the state of war that exists in the region.

Ladies and gentlemen, peace is not the putting of a signature under written lines. It is a new writing of history. Peace is not a competition in calling for peace so as to defend any greedy designs or to conceal any ambitions. In essence, peace is a mammoth struggle against all greedy designs and ambitions.

The experiences of past and contemporary history teach us all that missiles, warships and nuclear weapons, perhaps, cannot establish security. On the contrary, they destroy all that was built by security. For the sake of our peoples, for the sake of a civilization made by man, we must protect man in every place from the rule of the force of arms. We must raise high the rule of humanity with the full force of principles and values which hold man high.

If you will permit me to address an appeal from this platform to the people of Israel, I address a genuine sincere word to every man, woman and child in Israel, and tell them:

I bring to you from the people of Egypt who bless this sacred mission for peace, I bring to you the mission of peace, the mission of the Egyptian people who are not fanatics and whose sons, Moslems, Christians and Jews, live in a spirit of amity, love and tolerance. This is the Egypt whose people have entrusted me with carrying the sacred mission to you, the mission of security, hope and peace.

Every man and woman, every child in Israel, encourage your leaders to struggle for peace. Let all the efforts be directed towards the building of a mammoth edifice of peace instead of the building of fortresses and shelters fortified with missiles of destruction. Give to the whole world the picture of the new man in this part of the world so that he may be an example for the man of the age, the man of peace in every position and in every place. Give your children the good tidings that what has passed is the last of wars and the end of agonies, and that what is coming is the new beginning of the new life, the life of love and good, freedom and peace.

Mothers who have lost their sons, widowed wife, son who has lost a brother or a father, all victims of wars, fill the earth and space with the praise of peace. Fill the hearts and breasts with the hopes of peace.

Make the song a fact, one that lives and bears fruit. Make hope an article of work and struggle. The will of the peoples is from the will of God.

Ladies and gentlemen, before coming to his place, I turned with every pulse in my heart and every spark in my conscience to Almighty God while I performed the Id prayers in the Al-Aqsa Mosque and when I visited the Church of the Sepulchre – I turned to Almighty God praying to Him to grant the power and to strengthen my conviction that this visit should achieve its objectives, objectives I aspire to for the sake of a happy present and a happier future.

I have chosen to depart from all precedents and traditions known to countries at war and despite the fact that the Arab territory is still under occupation. Indeed, my announcement of my readiness to come to Israel was a big surprise which has upset many feelings, astounded many minds and aroused suspicions about what lies behind it. Despite all that, I took my decision in full, open and honest faith and with the full, true expression of the will and intentions of my people. I chose this hard path, which in the eyes of many is the hardest path.

I have chosen to come to you with an open heart and an open mind, to give this momentum to all the international efforts made to achieve peace. I have chosen to put forward to you, and in your own house, the real facts, free from any scheme or whim; not to conduct manoeuvres, or to gain a round, but in order that we may, together, win the most grave round and battle in contemporary history – the battle of a just and lasting peace. It is not just my battle, nor is it just the battle of leadership in Israel; it is truly the battle of all citizens of all our lands, who have the right to live in peace. It is a commitment of the conscience and responsibility in the hearts of millions of people.

When I put forward this initiative, many wondered about how I envisaged the achievements that could be reached by this visit, and about where I expected it to lead. Just as I have answered those who put questions to me, I declare before you that I did not think of making this initiative from the point of view of what could be achieved during the visit, but I have come here to deliver a message. Have I delivered the message? God be my witness. God, I repeat what Zakariah said: I love right and peace; and I take inspiration from what God has said in the Holy Book: 'Say: We believe in God, and in what God has sent down on us, and in what has been sent down on Ibrahim, Isma'il, Isaac, Jacob and the tribes and what was bestowed on Moses and the Christ and prophets by their God; we do not single out any of them, in whom we believe' [Koran]. God say the truth. Peace be upon you.

SWB, ME/5672/D/1 − 8

88   Prime Minister Begin's address to the Knesset, 20 November 1977

Mr Speaker, Mr President of the State of Israel, Mr President of the Arab Republic of Egypt, Ladies and Gentlemen, members of the Knesset, we send our greetings to the President, to all the people of the Islamic religion in our country, and wherever they may be, on this the occasion of the Feast, the Festival of the Sacrifice, Id al-Adha. This feast reminds us of the binding of Isaac. This was the way in which the Creator of the World tested our forefather, Abraham − our common forefather − to test his faith, and Abraham passed this test. However, from the moral aspect and the advancement of humanity it was forbidden to sacrifice human beings. Our two people in their ancient traditions know and taught what the Lord − Blessed be He − taught while people around us still sacrificed human beings to their gods. Thus we contributed, the people of Israel and the Arab people, to the progress of mankind, and thus we are continuing to contribute to human culture to this day.

I greet and welcome the President of Egypt for coming to our country and on his participating in the Knesset session. The flight time between Cairo and Jerusalem is short, but the distance between Cairo and Jerusalem was until last night almost endless. President Sadat crossed this distance courageously. We, the Jews, know how to appreciate such courage, and we know how to appreciate it in our guest, because it is with courage that we are here and this is how we continue to exist, and we shall continue to exist.

Mr Speaker, this small nation, the remaining refuge of the Jewish people which returned to its historic homeland − has always wanted peace and, since the dawn of our independence, on 14 May 1948 − 5th Iyar Tashah, in the Declaration of Independence in the founding scroll of our national freedom, David Ben Gurion said: We extend a hand of peace and good-neighbourliness to all the neighbouring countries and their peoples. We call upon them to cooperate, to help each other, with the Hebrew people independent in its own country. One year earlier, even from the underground, when we were in the midst of the fateful struggle for the liberation of the country and the redemption of the people, we called on our neighbours in these terms: In this country we shall live together and we shall advance together and we shall live of freedom and happiness. Our Arab neighbours: Do not reject the hand stretched out to you in peace.

But it is my bounden duty, Mr Speaker, and not only my right, not to pass over the truth, that our hand outstretched for peace was not grasped and, one day after we had renewed our independence — as was our right, our eternal right, which cannot be disputed — we were attacked on three fronts and we stood almost without arms, the few against many, the weak against the strong, while an attempt was made, one day after the Declaration of Independence, to strangle it at birth, to put an end to the last hope of the Jewish people, the yearning renewed after the years of destruction and holocaust.

No, we do not believe in might and we have never based our attitude to the Arab people on might; quite the contrary, force was used against us. Over all the years of this generation we have never stopped being attacked by might, the might of the strong arm stretched out to exterminate our people, to destroy our independence, to deny our rights. We defended ourselves, it is true. We defended our rights, our existence, our honour, our women and children, against these repeated and recurring attempts to crush us through the force of arms and not only on one front. That, too, is true. With the help of Almighty God, we overcame the forces of aggression, and we have guaranteed the existence of our nation, not only for this generation, but for the coming generations, too. We do not believe in might; we believe in right, only in right and therefore our aspiration, from the depth of our hearts, has always been, to this very day, for peace.

Mr President, Mr President of Egypt, the commanders of all the underground Hebrew fighting organizations are sitting in this democratic house. They had to conduct a campaign of the few against the many, against a huge, a world power. Here are sitting the veteran commanders and captains who had to go forth into battle because it was forced upon them and forward to victory which was unavoidable because they were defending their rights. They belong to different parties. They have different views, but I am sure, Mr President, that I am expressing the views of everyone with no exceptions, that we have one aspiration in our hearts, one desire in our souls and all of us are united in these aspirations and desires — to bring peace, peace for our nation, which has not known peace for even one day since we started returning to Zion, and peace for our neighbours, whom we wish all the best, and we believe that if we make peace, real peace, we shall be able to help our neighbours in all walks of life and a new era will open in the Middle East, an era of blossoming and growth, development and expansion of the economy, its growth as it was in the past.

Therefore, permit me, today, to set out the peace programme as we understand it. We want full, real peace, with complete reconciliation between the Jewish and the Arab peoples. I do not wish to dwell on the memories of the past but there have been wars; there has been blood spilt; wonderful young people have been killed on both sides. We shall live all our life with the memories of our heroes who gave their lives so this day would arrive, this day, too, would come, and we respect the bravery of a rival and we honour all the members of the younger generation among the Arabs who also fell.

I do not wish to dwell on memories of the past, although they are bitter memories. We shall bury them, we shall worry about the future, about our people, our children, our joint and common future. For it is true indeed that we shall have to live in this area, all of us together shall live here, for generations upon generations; the great Arab people in their various states and countries and the Jewish people in their country, Eretz Yisra'el. Therefore we must determine what peace means.

Let us conduct negotiations, Mr President, as free negotiating partners for a peace treaty and, with the aid of the Lord, we fully believe the day will come when we can sign it with mutual respect, and we shall then know that the era of wars is over, that hands have been extended between friends, that each has shaken the hand of his brother and the future will be shining for all the people of this area. The beginning of wisdom in a peace treaty is the abolition of the state of war. I agree, Mr President, that you did not come here, we did not invite you to our country, in order, as has been said in recent days, to divide the Arab people. Somebody quoted an ancient Roman saying: Divide and rule. Israel does not want to rule and therefore does not need to divide. We want peace with all our neighbours, with Egypt, with Jordan, with Syria and with Lebanon. We would like to negotiate peace treaties (at this point Tawfiq Toubi interrupts Begin). Mr President, my parliamentary colleague of the Communist Party has interrupted me but I am glad to this extent, he didn't interrupt you.

And there is no need to distinguish between a peace treaty and an abolition of the state of war. Quite the contrary, we are not proposing this nor are we asking for it. The first clause of a peace treaty is cessation of the state of war, for ever. We want to establish normal relations between us, as they exist between all nations, even after wars.

We have learned from history, Mr President, that war is avoidable, peace is unavoidable. Many nations have waged war between each other and sometimes they used the tragic term, a perennial enemy. There are no perennial enemies. And after the wars the inevitable comes — peace. And so we want to establish, in a peace treaty, diplomatic relations, as is the custom among civilized nations.

Today two flags are flying over Jerusalem — the Egyptian flag and the Israeli flag. And we saw together, Mr President, little children waving both the flags. Let us sign a peace treaty and let us establish this situation forever, both in Jerusalem and in Cairo, and I hope the day will come when the Egyptian children wave the Israeli flag and the Egyptian flag just as the children of Israel waved both these flags in Jerusalem.

And you, Mr President, will have a loyal ambassador in Jerusalem and we shall have an ambassador in Cairo. And even if differences of opinion arise between us, we shall clarify them, like civilized peoples, through our authorized envoys.

We are proposing economic cooperation for the development of our countries. There are wonderful countries in the Middle East, the Lord created it thus: oases in the desert, but we can make the deserts flourish as well. Let us cooperate in this field, let us develop our countries, let us eliminate poverty, hunger, homelessness. Let us raise our peoples to the level of developed countries, let them call us developing countries no longer.

With all due respect, I am willing to repeat the words of His Majesty, the King of Morocco who said in public that if peace came about in the Middle East, the combination of Arab genius and Jewish genius together could turn this area into a paradise on earth.

Let us open our countries to free traffic. You come to our country and we shall visit yours. I am ready to announce, Mr Speaker, this very day, that our country is open to the citizens of Egypt, and I make no conditions. I think it is only proper and just that there should be a joint announcement on this matter. But just as there are Egyptian flags in our streets, and there is an honoured delegation from Egypt in our country, in our capital, let the number of visitors increase, our border with you will be open, as will all (our) other borders.

As I pointed out, we want this in the south, in the north, in the east; so I am renewing my invitation to the President of Syria to follow in your footsteps, Mr President, and come to us to open negotiations for a peace between Israel and Syria, so that we may sign a peace treaty between us. I am sorry but I must say that there is no justification for the mourning they have declared beyond our northern border. Quite the contrary, such visits, such links, such clarifications can and must be days of joy, days of the raising of spirits of all people. I invite King Husayn to come to us to discuss all the problems which need to be discussed between us. And genuine representatives of the Arabs of Eretz Yisra'el, I invite them to come and hold clarification talks with us about our common future, about guaranteeing the freedom of man, social justice, peace, mutual respect. And if they invite us to come to their capitals, we shall accept their invitations. If they invite us to open negotiations in Damascus, in Amman or in Beirut, we shall go to those capitals in order to hold negotiations with them there. We do not want to divide; we want real people with all our neighbours, to be expressed in peace treaties whose contents I have already made clear.

Mr Speaker, it is my duty today to tell our guest and the peoples watching us and listening to our words about the link between our people and this land. The President [of Egypt] recalled the Balfour Declaration. No, sir, we did not take over any strange land; we returned to our homeland. The link between our people and this land is eternal. It arose in the earliest days of the history of humanity and was never altered. In this country we developed our civilization. We had our prophets here and their sacred words stand to this day. Here the Kings of Judah and Israel knelt before their God. This is where we became a people, here we established our Kingdom. And when we were expelled from our land, when force was used against us, no matter how far we went from our land, we never forgot it for even one day. We prayed for it, we longed for it, we believed in our return to it from the day these words were spoken: When the Lord restores the fortunes of Zion, we shall be like dreamers. Our mouths will be filled with laughter, and our tongues will speak with shouts of joy. These verses apply to all our exiles and all our sufferings, giving us the consolation that the return to Zion would come.

This, our right, was recognized. The Balfour Declaration was included in the mandate laid down by the nations of the world, including the United States of America, and the preface to this recognized international document says: Whereas recognition has the bible given to the historical connection of the Jewish people with Palestine and to the grounds for reconstituting their national home in that country the historic connection between the Jewish people and Palestine or, in Hebrew, Eretz Yisra'el, was given recon-firmation — reconfirmation — as the national homeland in that country, that is, in Eretz Yisra'el.

In 1919 we also won recognition of this right by the spokesman of the

Arab people and the agreement of 3 January 1919, which was signed by Prince Faysal and Chaim Weizmann. It reads: Mindful of the racial kinship and ancient bonds existing between the Arabs and the Jewish people and realizing that the surest means of working out the consummation of the national aspirations is the closest possible collaboration in the development of the Arab State and of Palestine. And afterwards come all the clauses about cooperation between the Arab state and Eretz Yisra'el. That is our right. The existence – truthful existence.

What happened to us when our homeland was taken from us? I accompanied you this morning, Mr President, to Yad Vashem.[1] With your own eyes you saw the fate of our people when this homeland was taken from it. It cannot be told. Both of us agreed, Mr President, that anyone who has seen with his own eyes everything there is in Yad Vashem cannot understand what happened to this people when it was without a homeland, when its own homeland was taken from it. And both of us read a document dated 30 January 1939, where the word 'vernichtung' – annihilation – appears. If war breaks out, the Jewish race in Europe will be exterminated. Then, too, we were told that we should not pay attention to the racists. The whole world heard. Nobody came to save us. Not during the nine fateful, decisive months after the announcement was made, the like of which had not been seen since the Lord created man and man created the Devil.

And during those six years, too, when millions of our people, among them one and a half million of the little children of Israel who were burnt on all the strange beds, nobody came to save them, not from the East and not from the West. And because of this, we took a solemn oath, this entire generation – the generation of extermination and revival – that we would never again put our people in danger, that we would never again put our women and children, whom it is our duty to defend – if there is a need of this, even at the cost of our lives – in the Hell of the exterminating fire of an enemy. It is our duty for generations to come to remember that certain things said about our people must be taken with complete seriousness. And we must not, Heaven forbid, for the sake of the future of our people, accept any advice whatsoever against taking these things seriously.

President Sadat knows and he knew from us before he came to Jerusalem that we have a different position from his with regard to the permanent borders between us and our neighbouts. However, I say to

1   Memorial at Jerusalem to the Jews murdered by the Nazis.

the President of Egypt and to all our neighbours: Do not say there is not, there will not be negotiations about any particular issue. I propose, with the agreement of the decisive majority of this parliament, that everything be open to negotiation. Anyone who says, with reference to relations between the Arab people, or the Arab peoples around us, and the State of Israel, that there are things which should be omitted from negotiations is taking upon himself a grave responsibility, everything can be negotiated. No side will say the contrary. No side will present prior conditions. We shall conduct the negotiations honourably. If there are differences of opinion between us, this is not unusual, Anyone who has studied the history of wars and the signing of peace treaties knows that all negotiations over a peace treaty began with differences of opinion between the sides. And in the course of the negotiations they came to an agreement which permitted the signing of peace treaties and agreements. And this is the road we propose to take.

SWB, ME/5672/8 – 12

89   President Carter's news conference, 17 August 1978

All of us were pleased last November (and December) when the exchange of visits took place—Sadat going to Jerusalem, Begin going to Ismailia. It was one of the happiest few weeks of my career as President not to be involved in these negotiations and to see them face-to-face, trying to work out the differences between them.

Since then, the interrelationships which brought us such high hopes last winter have deteriorated rapidly. In spite of our best efforts, recently, those peace talks broke down completely, not only at the high level of the Prime Minister and President but even at a lower level involving cabinet officers themselves. Even when Secretary Vance had scheduled a trip to the Mideast, we could not get the leaders to agree to meet.

It is a very high-risk for me politically, because now I think if we are unsuccessful at Camp David, I will certainly have to share part of the blame for that failure. But I don't see that I could do anything differently, because I'm afraid that if the leaders do not meet and do not permit their subordinates to meet in a continuing series of tough negotiations that the situation in the Middle East might be much more serious in the future even than it is now.

DSB, vol. 78, no. 2019, October 1978

90   'Framework for the Conclusion of a Peace Between Egypt and Israel', Camp David, 17 September 1978

In order to achieve peace between them, Israel and Egypt agree to negotiate in good faith with a goal of concluding within three months of the signing of this framework a peace treaty between them.

It is agreed that:

The site of the negotiations will be under a United Nations flag at a location or locations to be mutually agreed.

All of the principles of UN Resolution 242 will apply in this resolution of the dispute between Israel and Egypt.

Unless otherwise mutually agreed, terms of the peace treaty will be implemented between two and three years after the peace treaty is signed.

The following matters are agreed between the parties:

(a) the full exercise of Egyptian sovereignty up to the internationally recognized border between Egypt and mandated Palestine;

(b) the withdrawal of Israeli armed forces from the Sinai;

(c) the use of airfields left by the Israelis near El Arish, Rafah, Ras en Naqb, and Sharm el Sheikh for civilian purposes only, including possible commercial use by all nations;

(d) the right of free passage by ships of Israel through the Gulf of Suez and the Suez Canal on the basis of the Constantinople Convention of 1888 applying to all nations; the Strait of Tiran and the Gulf of Aqaba are international waterways to be open to all nations for unimpeded and nonsuspendable freedom of navigation and overflight;

(e) the construction of a highway between the Sinai and Jordan near Elath with guaranteed free and peaceful passage by Egypt and Jordan; and

(f) the stationing of military forces listed below.

STATIONING OF FORCES

A   No more than one division (mechanized or infantry) of Egyptian armed forces will be stationed within an area lying approximately 50 kilometres (km) east of the Gulf of Suez and the Suez Canal.

B   Only United Nations forces and civil police equipped with light weapons to perform normal police functions will be stationed within an area lying west of the international border and the Gulf of Aqaba, varying in width from 20 km to 40km.

C   In the area within 3 km east of the international border there will be Israeli limited military forces not to exceed four infantry battalions and United Nations observers.

D   Border patrol units, not to exceed three battalions, will supplement the civil police in maintaining order in the area not included above.

The exact demarcation of the above areas will be as decided during the peace negotiations.

Early warning stations may exist to insure compliance with the terms of the agreement.

United Nations forces will be stationed: (a) in part of the area in the Sinai lying within about 20 km to the Mediterranean Sea and adjacent to the international border, and (b) in the Sharm el Sheikh area to insure freedom of passage through the Straits of Tiran; and these forces will not be removed unless such removal is approved by the Security Council of the United Nations with a unanimous vote of the five permanent members.

After a peace treaty is signed, and after the interim withdrawal is complete, normal relations will be established between Egypt and Israel, including: full recognition, including diplomatic, economic and cultural relations; termination of economic boycotts and barriers to the free movement of goods and people; and mutual protection of citizens by the due process of law.

INTERIM WITHDRAWAL

Between three months and nine months after the signing of the peace treaty, all Israeli forces will withdraw east of a line extending from a point east of El Arish to Ras Muhammad, the exact location of this line to be determined by mutual agreement.

DSB, vol. 78, no. 2019, October 1978

91   'A Framework for Peace in the Middle East agreed at Camp David', 17 September 1978

Muhammad Anwar al-Sadat, President of the Arab Republic of Egypt, and Menachem Begin, Prime Minister of Israel, met with Jimmy Carter, President of the United States of America, at Camp David from 5 September to 17 September 1978, and have agreed on the following framework for peace in the Middle East. They invite other parties to the Arab-Israeli conflict to adhere to it.

PREAMBLE

The search for peace in the Middle East must be guided by the following:

● The agreed basis for a peaceful settlement of the conflict between Israel and its neighbors is United Nations Security Council Resolution 242, in all its parts.

● After four wars during thirty years, despite intensive human efforts, the Middle East, which is the cradle of civilization and the birthplace of three great religions, does not yet enjoy the blessings of peace. The people of the Middle East yearn for peace so that the vast human and natural resources of the region can be turned to the pursuits of peace and so that this area can become a model for coexistence and cooperation among nations.

● The historic initiative of President Sadat in visiting Jerusalem and the reception accorded to him by the Parliament, government and people of Israel, and the reciprocal visit of Prime Minister Begin to Ismailia, the peace proposals made by both leaders, as well as the warm reception of these missions by the peoples of both countries, have created an unprecedented opportunity for peace which must not be lost if this generation and future generations are to be spared the tragedies of war.

● The provisions of the Charter of the United Nations and the other accepted norms of international law and legitimacy now provide accepted standards for the conduct of relations among all states.

● To achieve a relationship of peace, in the spirit of Article 2 of the United Nations Charter, future negotiations between Israel and any neighbor prepared to negotiate peace and security with it, are necessary for the purpose of carrying out all the provisions and principles of Resolutions 242 and 338.

● Peace requires respect for the sovereignty, territorial integrity and political independence of every state in the area and their right to live in peace within secure and recognized boundaries free from threats or acts of force. Progress toward that goal can accelerate movement toward a new era of reconciliation in the Middle East marked by cooperation in promoting economic development, in maintaining stability, and in assuring security.

● Security is enhanced by a relationship of peace and by cooperation between nations which enjoy normal relations. In addition, under the terms of peace treaties, the parties can, on the basis of reciprocity, agree to special security arrangements such as demilitarized zones, limited armaments areas, early warning stations, the presence of international forces, liaison, agreed measures for monitoring, and other arrangements that they agree are useful.

FRAMEWORK

Taking these factors into account, the parties are determined to reach a just, comprehensive, and durable settlement of the Middle East conflict through the conclusion of peace treaties based on Security Council Resolutions 242 and 338 in all their parts. Their purpose is to achieve peace and good neighborly relations. They recognize that, for peace to endure, it must involve all those who have been most deeply affected by the conflict. They therefore agree that this framework as appropriate is intended by them to constitute a basis for peace not only between Egypt and Israel, but also between Israel and each of its other neighbors which is prepared to negotiate peace with Israel on this basis. With that objective in mind, they have agreed to proceed as follows:

A WEST BANK AND GAZA

1   Egypt, Israel, Jordan and the representatives of the Palestinian people should participate in negotiations on the resolution of the Palestinian problem in all its aspects. To achieve that objective, negotiations relating to the West Bank and Gaza should proceed in three stages:

(a) Egypt and Israel agree that, in order to ensure a peaceful and orderly transfer of authority, and taking into account the security concerns of all the parties, there should be transitional arrangements for the West Bank and Gaza for a period not exceeding five years. In order to provide full autonomy to the inhabitants, under these arrangements the Israeli military government and its civilian administration will be withdrawn as soon as a self-governing authority has been freely elected by the inhabitants of these areas to replace the existing military government. To negotiate the details of a transitional arrangement, the Government of Jordan will be invited to join the negotiations on the basis of this framework. These new arrangements should give due consideration both to the principle of self-government by the inhabitants of these territories and to the legitimate security concerns of the parties involved.

(b) Egypt, Israel, and Jordan will agree on the modalities for establishing the elected self-governing authorities in the West Bank and Gaza. The delegations of Egypt and Jordan may include

Palestinians from the West Bank and Gaza or other Palestinians as mutually agreed. The parties will negotiate an agreement which will define the powers and responsibilities of the self-governing authority to be exercised in the West Bank and Gaza. A withdrawal of Israeli armed forces will take place and there will be a redeployment of the remaining Israeli forces into specified security locations. The agreement will also include arrangements for assuring internal and external security and public order. A strong local police force will be established, which may include Jordanian citizens. In addition, Israeli and Jordanian forces will participate in joint patrols and in the manning of control posts to assure the security of the borders.

(c) When the self-governing authority (administrative council) in the West Bank and Gaza is established and inaugurated, the transitional period of five years will begin. As soon as possible, but not later than the third year after the beginning of the transitional period, negotiations will take place to determine the final status of the West Bank and Gaza and its relationship with its neighbors, and to conclude a peace treaty between Israel and Jordan by the end of the transitional period. These negotiations will be conducted among Egypt, Israel, Jordan, and the elected representatives of the inhabitants of the West Bank and Gaza. Two separate but related committees will be convened, one committee, consisting of representatives of the four parties which will negotiate and agree on the final status of the West Bank and Gaza, and its relationship with its neighbors, and the second committee, consisting of representatives of Israel and representatives of Jordan to be joined by the elected representatives of the inhabitants of the West Bank and Gaza, to negotiate the peace treaty between Israel and Jordan, taking into account the agreement reached on the final status of the West Bank and Gaza. The negotiations will be based on all the provisions and principles of UN Security Council Resolution 242. The negotiations will resolve, among other matters, the location of the boundaries and the nature of the security arrangements. The solution from the negotiations must also recognize the legitimate rights of the Palestinian people and their just requirements. In this way, the Palestinians will participate in the determination of their own future through:

(1) The negotiations among Egypt, Israel, Jordan and the representatives of the inhabitants of the West Bank and Gaza to agree on the final status of the West Bank and Gaza and other outstanding issues by the end of the transitional period.

(2) Submitting their agreement to a vote by the elected representatives of the inhabitants of the West Bank and Gaza.

(3)   Providing for the elected representatives of the inhabitants of the West Bank and Gaza to decide how they shall govern themselves consistent with the provisions of their agreement.

(4)   Participating as stated above in the work of the committee negotiating the peace treaty between Israel and Jordan.

2   All necessary measures will be taken and provisions made to assure the security of Israel and its neighbors during the transitional period and beyond. To assist providing such security, a strong local police force will be constituted by the self-governing authority. It will be composed of inhabitants of the West Bank and Gaza. The police will maintain continuing liaison on internal security matters with the designated Israeli, Jordanian, and Egyptian officers.

3   During the transitional period, representatives of Egypt, Israel, Jordan, and the self-governing authority will constitute a continuing committee to decide by agreement on the modalities of admission of persons displaced from the West Bank and Gaza in 1967, together with necessary measures to prevent disruption and disorder. Other matters of common concern may also be dealt with by this committee.

4   Egypt and Israel will work with each other and with other interested parties to establish agreed procedures for a prompt, just and permanent implementation of the resolution of the refugee problem.

B   EGYPT-ISRAEL

1   Egypt and Israel undertake not to resort to the threat or the use of force to settle disputes. Any disputes shall be settled by peaceful means in accordance with Article 33 of the Charter of the United Nations.

2   In order to achieve peace between them, the parties agree to negotiate in good faith with a goal of concluding within three months from the signing of this Framework a peace treaty between them, while inviting the other parties to the conflict to proceed simultaneously to negotiate and conclude similar peace treaties with a view to achieving a comprehensive peace in the area. The Framework for the Conclusion of a Peace Treaty Between Egypt and Israel will govern the peace negotiations between them. The parties will agree on the modalities and the timetable for the implementation of their obligations under the treaty.

C   ASSOCIATED PRINCIPLES

1   Egypt and Israel state that the principles and provisions described below should apply to peace treaties between Israel and each of its neighbors—Egypt, Jordan, Syria and Lebanon.

2   Signatories shall establish among themselves relationships normal

to states at peace with one another. To this end, they should undertake to abide by all the provisions of the Charter of the United Nations. Steps to be taken in this respect include:

(a) full recognition;

(b) abolishing economic boycotts;

(c) guaranteeing that under their jurisdiction the citizens of the other parties shall enjoy the protection of the due process of law.

3   Signatories should explore possibilities for economic development in the context of final peace treaties, with the objective of contributing to the atmosphere of peace, cooperation and friendship which is their common goal.

4   Claims Commissions may be established for the mutual settlement of all financial claims.

5   The United States shall be invited to participate in the talks on matters related to the modalities of the implementation of the agreements and working out the timetable for the carrying out of the obligations of the parties.

6   The United Nations Security Council shall be requested to endorse the peace treaties and ensure that their provisions shall not be violated. The permanent members of the Security Council shall be requested to underwrite the peace treaties and ensure respect for their provisions. They shall also be requested to conform their policies and actions with the undertaking contained in this Framework.

                                        DSB, vol. 78, no. 2019, October 1978

92 Proclamation of the Steadfastness Front, Damascus, 23 September 1978

The Heads of State of the Democratic People's Republic of Algeria, the Syrian Arab Republic, the Socialist People's Libyan Arab Jamahiriyah and the People's Democratic Republic of Yemen, and the Chairman of the Palestine Liberation Organization meeting in Damascus from 18 to 21 shawwal 1398 AH, corresponding to 20 and 23 September 1978, after studying the current Arab situation, particularly the results stemming from the signing by the head of the Egyptian regime of the two Camp David agreements and their supplements; and proceeding from the principles they approved at the Tripoli and Algiers summit conferences; and out of commitment to their pan-Arab responsibilities, have taken several resolutions. These resolutions are:

1   To break off political and economic relations with the Egyptian

regime, including Egyptian establishments and companies, and to apply the decisions of the Arab boycott of Israel to all individuals dealing with the enemy.

2   To work to transfer the headquarters of the Arab League and its various organizations from Cairo. If this is not achieved, then the sides participating and the pan-Arab states cooperating with them, will carry out the tasks of the Arab League in accordance with the Arab League Charter and goals. In this case, the headquarters of the Arab League will be in an Arab country other than Egypt.

3   To support the struggle of the Egyptian people, represented in their nationalist and progressive forces, to cope with the plotting of the Egyptian regime against the fateful Arab issue.

4   To entrust President Hafiz al-Asad with the task of making a tour of Arab states in order to explain the resolutions of the summit conference of steadfastness and confrontation, to work for gaining maximum Arab political and material support for these resolutions and to discuss the possibility of convening an Arab summit conference without the participation of the Egyptian regime.

5   To empower President Hafiz al-Asad to contact the Soviet Union in the name of the front to discuss the possibility of developing relations between the Soviet Union and the front which would lead to giving more military and political support, restoring the balance of military and political power in the area and strengthening and deepening friendship between the Soviet Union and the member states of the front.

6   To send a collective memorandum in the name of the front to the non-aligned group, to the general secretariat of the Islamic Congress, and to the OAU[1] explaining the front's position.

7   To invite the UN committee in charge of securing the Palestinian people's constant national rights to hold a special meeting to study the Camp David documents and to determine their contradictions concerning the rights of the Palestine people, and to ask the committee to issue a statement asserting the committee's objection to everything that harms or belittles those rights.[2]

8   To request the Secretary General of the United Nations to get the United Nations to refrain from approving any document or agreement that contradicts the UN resolutions on the Palestine issue and the

---

1   Organization of African Unity.
2   Committee on the Exercise of the Inalienable Rights of the Palestinian People, established by General Assembly Resolution 3376(XXX), 10 November 1975.

withdrawal from the occupied areas and to notify the Security Council on this matter.

SWB, ME/5925/A/10 – 11

93 Treaty of Peace between the Arab Republic of Egypt and the State of Israel, Washington, 26 March 1979

The Government of the Arab Republic of Egypt and the Government of the State of Israel;

PREAMBLE

Convinced of the urgent necessity of the establishment of a just, comprehensive and lasting peace in the Middle East in accordance with Security Council Resolutions 242 and 338.

Reaffirming their adherence to the 'Framework for Peace in the Middle East Agreed at Camp David', dated 17 September 1978.

Noting that the aforementioned Framework as appropriate is intended to constitute a basis for peace not only between Egypt and Israel but also between Israel and each of its other Arab neighbors which is prepared to negotiate peace with it on this basis;

Desiring to bring to an end the state of war between them and to establish a peace in which every state in the area can live in security;

Convinced that the conclusion of a Treaty of Peace between Egypt and Israel is an important step in the search for comprehensive peace in the area and for the attainment of the settlement of the Arab-Israeli conflict in all its aspects;

Inviting the other Arab parties to this dispute to join the peace process with Israel guided by and based on the principles of the aforementioned Framework;

Desiring as well to develop friendly relations and cooperation between themselves in accordance with the United Nations Charter and the principles of international law governing international relations in times of peace;

Agree to the following provisions in the free exercise of their sovereignty, in order to implement the 'Framework for the Conclusion of a Peace Treaty Between Egypt and Israel':

ARTICLE I

1   The state of war between the Parties will be terminated and peace

will be established between them upon the exchange of instruments of ratification of this Treaty.

2   Israel will withdraw all its armed forces and civilians from the Sinai behind the international boundary between Egypt and mandated Palestine, as provided for in the annexed protocol (Annex I), and Egypt will resume the exercise of its full sovereignty over the Sinai.

3   Upon completion of the interim withdrawal provided for in Annex I, the Parties will establish normal and friendly relations, in accordance with Article III(3).

ARTICLE II

The permanent boundary between Egypt and Israel is the recognized international boundary between Egypt and the former mandated territory of Palestine, as shown on the map at Annex II, without prejudice to the issue of the status of the Gaza Strip. The parties recognize this boundary as inviolable. Each will respect the territorial integrity of the other, including their territorial waters and airspace.

ARTICLE III

1   The Parties will apply between them the provisions of the Charter of the United Nations and the principles of international law governing relations among states in times of peace. In particular:

(a) they recognize and will respect each other's sovereignty, territorial integrity and political independence;

(b) They recognize and will respect each other's right to live in peace within their secure and recognized boundaries;

(c) They will refrain from the threat or use of force, directly or indirectly, against each other and will settle all disputes between them by peaceful means.

2   Each Party undertakes to ensure that acts or threats of belligerency, hostility, or violence do not originate from and are not committed from within its territory, or by any forces subject to its control or by any other forces stationed on its territory, against the population, citizens or property of the other Party. Each Party also undertakes to refrain from organizing, instigating, inciting, assisting or participating in acts or threats of belligerency, hostility, subversion or violence against the other Party, anywhere, and undertakes to ensure that perpetrators of such acts are brought to justice.

3   The Parties agree that the normal relationship established

between them will include full recognition, diplomatic, economic and cultural relations, termination of economic boycotts and discriminatory barriers to the free movement of people and goods, and will guarantee the mutual enjoyment of citizens of the due process of law. The process by which they undertake to achieve such a relationship parallel to the implementation of other provisions of this treaty is set out in the annexed protocol (Annex III).

ARTICLE IV

1   In order to provide maximum security for both Parties on the basis of reciprocity, agreed security arrangements will be established including limited force zones in Egyptian and Israeli territory, and United Nations forces and observers, described in detail as to nature and training in Annex I, and security arrangements the Parties may agree upon.

2   The Parties agree to the stationing of United Nations personnel in areas described in Annex I. The Parties agree not to request withdrawal of the United Nations personnel and that these personnel will not be removed unless such removal is approved by the Security Council of the United Nations, with the affirmitive vote of the five Permanent Members, unless the Parties otherwise agree.

3   A Joint Commission will be established to facilitate the implementation of the Treaty, as provided for in Annex I.

4   The security arrangements provided for in paragraphs 1 and 2 of this Article may at the request of either party be reviewed and amended by mutual agreement of the Parties.

ARTICLE V

1   Ships of Israel, and cargoes destined for or coming from Israel, shall enjoy the right of free passage through the Suez Canal and its approaches through the Gulf of Suez and the Mediterranean Sea on the basis of the Constantinople Convention of 1888, applying to all nations. Israeli nationals, vessels and cargoes destined for or coming from Israel, shall be accorded non-discriminatory treatment in all matters connected with usage of the canal.

2   The Parties consider the Strait of Tiran and the Gulf of Aqaba to be international waterways open to all nations for unimpeded and non-suspendable freedom of navigation and overflight. The Parties will respect each others' right to navigation and overflight for access to either country through the the Strait of Tiran and the Gulf of Aqaba.

ARTICLE VI

1   This Treaty does not affect and shall not be interpreted as affecting in any way the rights and obligations of the Parties under the Charter of the United Nations.

2   The Parties undertake to fulfill in good faith their obligations under this Treaty, without regard to action or inaction of any other party and independently of any instrument external to this Treaty.

3   They further undertake to take all the necessary measures for the application in their relations of the provisions of the multilateral conventions to which they are parties, including the submission of appropriate notification to the Secretary General of the United Nations and other depositories of such conventions.

4   The Parties undertake not to enter into any obligation in conflict with this Treaty.

5   Subject to Article 103 of the United Nations Charter, in the event of a conflict between the obligations of the Parties under the present Treaty and any of their other obligations, the obligations under this Treaty will be binding and implemented.

ARTICLE VII

1   Disputes arising out of the application or interpretation of this Treaty shall be resolved by negotiations.

2   Any such disputes which cannot be settled by negotiations shall be resolved by conciliation or submitted to arbitration.

ARTICLE VIII

The Parties agree to establish a claims commission for the mutual settlement of all financial claims.

ARTICLE IX

1   This Treaty shall enter into force upon exchange of instruments of ratification.

2   This Treaty supersedes the Agreement between Egypt and Israel of September, 1975.

3   All protocols, annexes, and maps attached to this Treaty shall be regarded as an integral part hereof.

4   The Treaty shall be communicated to the Secretary General of the United Nations for registration in accordance with the provisions of Article 102 of the Charter of the United Nations.

Done at Washington, DC, this 26th day of March, 1979, in triplicate in the English, Arabic, and Hebrew languages, each text being equally authentic. In case of any divergence of interpretation, the English text shall prevail.

·   ·   ·

Dear President Carter,

This letter confirms that Egypt and Israel have agreed as follows:

The Governments of Egypt and Israel recall that they concluded at Camp David and signed at the White House on 17 September 1978, the annexed documents entitled 'A Framework for Peace in the Middle East Agreed at Camp David' and 'Framework for the Conclusion of a Peace Treaty between Egypt and Israel'.

For the purpose of achieving a comprehensive peace settlement in accordance with the above-mentioned Framework, Egypt and Israel will proceed with the implementation of those provisions relating to the West Bank and the Gaza Strip. They have agreed to start negotiations within a month after the exchange of the instruments of ratification of the peace treaty. In accordance with the 'Framework for Peace in the Middle East', the Hashemite Kingdom of Jordan is invited to join the negotiations. The Delegations of Egypt and Jordan may include Palestinians from the West Bank and Gaza Strip or other Palestinians as mutually agreed.

The purpose of the negotiation shall be to agree prior to the elections on the modalities for establishing the elected self-governing authority (Administrative Council), define its powers and responsibilities, and agree upon other related issues. In the event Jordan decides not to take part in the negotiations, the negotiations will be held by Israel and Egypt.

The two Governments agree to negotiate continuously and in good faith to conclude these negotiations at the earliest possible date. They also agree that the objective of the negotiations is the establishment of the self-governing authority in the West Bank and Gaza in order to provide full autonomy to the inhabitants.

Egypt and Israel set for themselves the goal of completing the negotiations within one year so that elections will be held as expeditiously as possible after agreement has been reached between the parties. The self-governing authority referred to in the 'Framework for Peace in the Middle East' will be established and inaugurated one month after it has been elected, at which time the transitional period of five years will begin. The Israeli military government and its civilian administration will then be withdrawn, to be replaced by the self-governing authority, as specified in the 'Framework for Peace in the Middle East'. A withdrawal of Israeli armed forces will then take place and there will be redeployment of the remaining Israeli forces into specified security locations.

This letter also confirms our understanding that the United States Government will participate fully in all stages of negotiations.

> Sincerely yours,
> Mohamed Anwar El-Sadat
> Menachem Begin
>
> State Information Service, Arab Republic of Egypt

XI

The Rise of Middle Eastern Oil Power

The Organization of the Petroleum Exporting Countries (OPEC), whose actions have transformed the Middle Eastern and world economies since 1973, came into existence in 1960 as a mechanism whereby exporting countries might defend their interests against the power of the international oil companies. In 1959 and again in the following year, the companies significantly reduced the posted price for Middle Eastern and Venezuelan oil, the reaction being the formation of OPEC at Baghdad (94). From the beginning, the exporters knew that their oil was a wasting asset, whose development intimately affected their economic progress. The need to safeguard their vital natural resource underpinned their 'Statement of Petroleum Policy' in 1968 (95), even though they were still trying to formulate the techniques necessary to implement it.

By early 1973, however, OPEC members, now greatly expanded from the five original Baghdad signatories, were much more aware that they possessed an economic weapon of formidable potential. At Tehran in 1971, Saudi Arabia, Iraq and Iran had successfully increased the price for Arabian light crude oil, the 'marker crude' which determined the overall pricing structure, from $1.80 to $2.80 a barrel, with built-in increments to allow for inflation. World demand seemed unaffected by this and United States became an importer of Middle Eastern oil to compensate for the shortfall in her own production.

At a series of conferences in Vienna from 27 June to 27 September 1973, OPEC members evolved a more aggressive pricing policy, whereby oil prices would henceforward be related to their own plans for economic growth (96) and be compatible with prevailing market conditions (97, 98). But with the outbreak of war on 6 October, Middle Eastern oil power of a different nature came to be exerted. At Kuwait on 17 October, the members of the Organization of Arab Petroleum Exporting Countries (OAPEC) resolved to use their economic influence in support of Egypt, Syria and the Palestinians (**99**), announcing cuts in production. Frustrated by the lack of progress, a further OAPEC conference on 5 November (**100**) imposed more draconian cuts, reducing their production by 25 per cent of September's total.

The seal was put on this assertion of Middle Eastern economic power at further OPEC meetings on 20 November and 24 December (**101, 102**), which implemented previous conference decisions by allowing Arabian light crude to reach $11.651 a barrel, an increase to be set against the early October figure of $3.011. The cumulative economic consequences of these actions for the industrialized and, more especially, the underdeveloped countries were painful, but for the Arab oil producing states of the Middle East they gave vastly accelerated growth along with a considerably enhanced diplomatic influence (**85**).

The hard-won unity of OPEC, which had done so much to bring about these revolutionary changes for its Middle Eastern members, began noticeably to disintegrate within a few years. The economic and social interests of the Arab oil exporting states, with their rich reserves and comparatively small populations, were different from those of OPEC members with less favoured circumstances elsewhere in the world. Moreover, the Iranian revolution of 1979 introduced a new, and for a time unpredictable, variable into the oil supply situation. At the final OPEC conference of the decade, at Caracas in December 1979, these conflicting tensions surfaced to produce prices which were high but no longer coherent. Saudi Arabian light, the former 'marker crude', was now priced at $24.42 a barrel, while other Middle Eastern prices ranged from $21.43 on the part of Kuwait to Libya's $30.00. With prices being paid on the Rotterdam 'spot' market by certain industrialized nations reportedly reaching in excess of $40.00 a barrel, the 1980s promised to be yet another period of complex adjustment to the Middle East's dominant position in the world oil industry.

94   Resolutions of the first OPEC conference held in Baghdad, 10 – 14 September 1960.

By invitation of the Republic of Iraq, the Conference of the Petroleum Exporting Countries, composed of representatives of the Governments of Iran, Kuwait, Saudi Arabia and Venezuela, hereafter called Members, met at Baghdad from 10 to 14 September, 1960, and having considered:

That the Members are implementing much needed development programmes to be financed mainly from income derived from their petroleum exports;

That Members must rely on petroleum income to a large degree in order to balance their annual national budgets;

That Petroleum is a wasting asset and to the extent that it is depleted must be replaced by other assets;

That all nations of the world, in order to maintain and improve their standards of living must rely almost entirely on petroleum as a primary source of energy generation;

That any fluctuation in the price of petroleum necessarily affects the implementation of the Member's programmes and results in a dislocation detrimental not only to their own consumers but also to those of all consuming nations

have decided to adopt the following resolutions:

RESOLUTION I.1

1   That Members can no longer remain indifferent to the attitude heretofore adopted by the Oil Companies in effecting price modifications;

2   That Members shall demand that Oil Companies maintain their prices steady and free from all unnecessary fluctuations; that Members shall endeavour, by all means available to them, to restore present prices to the levels prevailing before the reductions; that they shall ensure that if any new circumstances arise which in the estimation of the Oil Companies necessitate price modifications, the said Companies shall enter into consultation with the Member or Members affected in order fully to explain the situation.

3   That Members shall study and formulate a system to ensure the stablization of prices by, among other means, the regulation of production, with due regard to the interests of the producing, and of the consuming nations and to the necessity of securing a steady income to the producing countries, an efficient, economic and regular supply of this source of energy to consuming nations, and a fair return on their capital to those investing in the petroleum industry;

4   That if as a result of the application of any unanimous decision of the Conference any sanctions are employed, directly or indirectly, by any interested Company against one or more of the Member Countries, no other Member shall accept any offer of a beneficial treatment, whether in the form of an increase in exports or an

improvement in prices which may be made to it by any such Company or Companies with the intention of discouraging the application of the unanimous decision reached by the Conference.

RESOLUTION I.2

1   With a view to giving effect to the provisions of Resolution I.1 the Conference decides to form a permanent Organization called the Organization of the Petroleum Exporting Countries, for regular consultation among its Members with a view to coordinating and unifying the policies of the Members and determining among other matters the attitude which Members should adopt whenever circumstances such as those referred to in Paragraph 2 of Resolution I.1 have arisen.

2   Countries represented in this Conference shall be the original Members of the Organization of the Petroleum Exporting Countries.

3   Any country with a substantial net export of crude petroleum can become a new Member if unanimously accepted by all five original Members of the Organization.[1]

4   The principal aim of the Organization shall be the unification of petroleum policies for the Member Countries and the determination of the best means for safeguarding the interests of Member Countries individually and collectively.

OPEC records, Vienna

95 'Declaratory Statement of Petroleum Policy in Member Countries', OPEC Resolution XVI.90, 25 June 1968

The Conference, recalling Paragraph 4 of its Resolution 1.2; recognizing that hydrocarbon resources in Member Countries are one of the principal sources of their revenues and foreign exchange earnings and therefore constitute the main basis for their economic development; bearing in mind that hydrocarbon resources are limited and exhaustible and that their proper exploitation determines the conditions of the economic development of Member Countries, both at present and in the future; bearing in mind also that the inalienable right of all countries to exercise permanent sovereignty over their natural resources in the interest of their national development is a universally recognized principle of public law and has been repeatedly

1   Algeria, Ecuador, Gabon, Indonesia, Libya, Nigeria, Qatar, and the United Arab Emirates were subsequently accepted for membership.

reaffirmed by the General Assembly of the United Nations, most notably in its Resolution 2158 of 25 November 1966; considering also that in order to ensure the exercise of permanent sovereignty over hydrocarbon resources, it is essential that their exploitation should be aimed at securing the greatest possible benefit for Member Countries; considering further that this aim can better be achieved if Member Countries are in a position to undertake themselves directly the exploitation of their hydrocarbon resources, so that they may exercise their freedom of choice in the utilization of hydrocarbon resources under the most favourable conditions; taking into account the fact that foreign capital, whether public or private, forthcoming at the request of the Member Countries, can play an important role, inasmuch as it supplements the efforts undertaken by them for the exploitation of their hydrocarbon resources, provided that there is government supervision of the activity of foreign capital to ensure that it is used in the interest of national development and that returns earned by it do not exceed reasonable levels; bearing in mind that the principal aim of the Organization, as set out in Article 2 of its Statute, 'is the coordination and unification of the petroleum policies of Member Countries and the determination of the best means for safeguarding their interests, both individually and collectively'; recommends that the following principles shall serve as basis for petroleum policy in Member Countries.

MODE OF DEVELOPMENT

1   Member Governments shall endeavour, as far as feasible, to explore for and develop their hydrocarbon resources directly. The capital, specialists and the promotion of marketing outlets required for such direct development may be complemented when necessary from alternate sources on a commercial basis.

2   However, when a Member Government is not capable of developing its hydrocarbon resources directly, it may enter into contracts of various types, to be defined in its legislation but subject to the present principles, with outside operations for a reasonable remuneration, taking into account the degree of risk involved. Under such an arrangement, the Government shall seek to retain the greatest possible measure of participation in and control over all aspects of operations.

3   In any event, the terms and conditions of such contracts shall be open to revision at predetermined intervals, as justified by changing circumstances. Such changing circumstances should call for the revision of existing concession agreements.

PARTICIPATION

Where provision for Government participation in the ownership of the concession-holding company under any of the present petroleum contracts has not been made, the Government may acquire a reasonable participation, on the grounds of the principle of changing circumstances.

If such provision has actually been made but avoided by the operators concerned, the rate provided for shall serve as a minimum basis for the participation to be acquired.

RELINQUISHMENT

A schedule of progressive and more accelerated relinquishment of acreage of present contract areas shall be introduced. In any event, the Government shall participate in the choosing the acreage to be relinquished, including those cases where relinquishment is already provided for but left to the decision of the operator.

POSTED PRICES OR TAX REFERENCE PRICES

All contracts shall require that the assessment of the operator's income, and its taxes or any other payments to the State, be based on a posted or tax reference price for the hydrocarbons produced under the contract. Such price shall be determined by the Government and shall move in such a manner as to prevent any deterioration in its relationship to the prices of manufactured goods traded internationally. However, such price shall be consistent, subject to differences in gravity, quality and geographic location, with the levels of posted or tax reference prices generally prevailing for hydrocarbons in other OPEC countries and accepted by them as a basis for tax payments.

.   .   .

RENEGOTIATION CLAUSE

Notwithstanding any guarantee of fiscal stability that may have been granted to the operator, the operation shall not have the right to obtain excessively high net earnings after taxes. The financial provisions of contracts which actually results in such excessively high net earnings shall be open to renegotiation.

.   .   .

CONSERVATION

Operators shall be required to conduct their operations in accordance with the best conservation practices, bearing in mind the long-term interests of the country. To this end, the Government shall draw up written instructions detailing the conservation rules to be followed generally by all contractors within its territory.

> OPEC *Annual Review and Record,* 1968, 16th OPEC Conference, 24 – 25 June 1968

96   OPEC Policy Statement, 28 June 1973

The Conference: noting that under the present and expected conditions of the world energy market, Member Countries should not only strive to attain the appropriate value for their oil, but should also negotiate with a view to attaining conditions that would effectively foster the permanent and diversified sources of income within their territories; taking into account that hydrocarbon resources have constituted an essential factor in the economic development of industrialized countries and that a regular and secure supply of hydrocarbons to these countries is of paramount importance for the continuity of their economic welfare; bearing in mind that petroleum should not only be a source of finance for the Member Countries but a primary and effective instrument for their economic development; noting that the inadequate economic conditions to which most developing countries are still subjected, mainly as a consequence of their lack of access to the markets and technology of the industrialized countries, hamper the developing possibilities of OPEC Member Countries and of the Third World in general; reiterating that hydrocarbon resources are of a limited and exhaustible nature and therefore their exploitation must be geared at attaining an accelerated and diversified development of Member Countries' economies; bearing in mind that one of the main aims of the Organization is to seek a just valorization of the hydrocarbon resources of Member Countries and the adequate protection of their revenues; bearing in mind that it is an objective of OPEC to secure a fair and equitable relationship between the producing-exporting countries and consuming-importing countries, and not inflict any damage to the world economy that could result from the interruption of hydrocarbon supplies; states;

1   that the exploitation and trade in hydrocarbons from Member

Countries should, in one form or another, be linked to the process of a rational and accelerated economic growth;

2   that any concerted action undertaken by industrialized-importing countries aimed at undermining OPEC's legitimate aspirations would only hamper the stable relations that have normally existed between these and OPEC Member Countries, and that to seek a direct confrontation with OPEC may have a damaging effect upon the world economy;

3   that the Governments of Member Countries should take, or pursue, whatever actions they should see fit in the appropriate bilateral or multilateral framework in order to:

(a) attain greater access to the technology and markets of the developed countries for their present and future industrial products; and

(b) further strengthen the cooperation with the oil importing-developing countries whose energy requirements are ever-increasing.

> OPEC Press Release. Resolutions of the
> XXXIV OPEC Conference, 27 – 28 June
> 1973, Resolution XXXIV.155

97   Decisions of the XXV Meeting (Extraordinary) of the OPEC Conference, 15 – 16 September 1973

The Conference heard and discussed the Report prepared by the Working Party which was set up in accordance with a decision taken by the XXXIV Ordinary Meeting of the Conference, regarding the proposed amendments to the Tehran, Tripoli and Lagos Agreements and decided that since the level of posted prices and the annual escalations provided for by those Agreements are no longer compatible with prevailing market conditions as well as the galloping world inflation, to negotiate individually or collectively with the representative of oil companies with a view to revising the terms of the said Agreements. The Member Countries of Abu Dhabi,[1] Iran, Iraq, Kuwait, Qatar and Saudi Arabia decided to negotiate collectively the revision of the terms of the Tehran Agreement with representatives of the oil companies on 8 October 1973, in Vienna.

---

1   In 1974 Abu Dhabi merged with the United Arab Emirates, which had come into being as an independent state in December 1971 on the ending of the United Kingdom's treaty relationships with Abu Dhabi, Ajman, Dubai, Fujairah, Ras al Khaimah, Sharjah and Umm al Qaiwain.

The Conference heard a statement by HE Mana Saeed Otaiba, Head of the Delegation of Abu Dhabi, to the effect that his country's crudes were not only generally underposted but their premium quality was not reflected in the posted prices, and decided to fully support Abu Dhabi in its endeavours to rectify che situation.

OPEC Press Release, 16 September 1973

98   Resolutions of the XXV Meeting (Extraordinary) of the OPEC Conference, 27 September 1973

The Conference, having examined the prevailing conditions and expected future trends of the crude oil and oil products markets, as well as the worldwide inflation, especially in the industrialized countries; having reviewed the terms of the Tehran, Tripoli and Lagos Agreements in the light of the above conditions and trends; *noting* that the present level of posted prices as determined by those Agreements is no longer compatible with such prevailing conditions and trends thus requiring an upward adjustment; *having noted* that the annual escalations provided for in those Agreements are also no longer in line with the current and expected future trends of world inflation, as well as the crude oil and product prices; *recognizing* that the oil companies are reaping high unearned profits owing to developments which have occurred since the conclusion of the Tehran, Tripoli and Lagos Agreements, and that such a situation is detrimental to the Member Countries leading to a further deterioration in the value of their oil; *resolves*

1   that the Member Countries concerned shall negotiate, individually or collectively, with the oil companies with a view to revising the Tehran, Tripoli and Lagos Agreements in the light of the prevailing conditions and expected future trends in the crude oil and oil product markets, as well as the world inflation;

2   to this end a ministerial Committee, composed of the Heads of Delegations of the Member Countries bordering the Gulf, be established in order to negotiate collectively the revision of the terms of the Tehran Agreement with the representatives of the oil companies, on the 8th of October, 1973, in Vienna; and

3   to empower the said Committee to call for an Extraordinary Meeting of the Conference if it is deemed necessary.

OPEC Press Release, 27 September 1973

99   Statement of the Ministerial Council of OAPEC, Kuwait, 17 October 1973

The Arab oil exporting countries are contributing to the world's prosperity, welfare and economy by exporting quantities of this vital natural wealth. Although the production of many of these states has exceeded the limit required by their local economy and the needs of their future generations for energy and sources of income, they have continued to increase their production, sacrificing their own interests for the sake of international cooperation and the interests of the consumers.

It is known that Israel occupied by force vast areas of three Arab states in the June 1967 war, and it is continuing its occupation heedless of the UN resolutions and the various appeals for peace from Arab and peace-loving states. Although the world community is committed to implementing the UN resolutions and preventing the aggressor from reaping the fruits of his aggression and seizing the lands of others by force, most of the great industrial states that consume Arab oil have not adopted any measure or action to indicate their awareness of this general international commitment; some of them, rather, have acted in a manner which supports and strengthens aggression.

The United States has been active before and during the current war, supplying Israel with all the sources of strength which increase its arrogance and enable it to defy legitimate rights and principles of general international law which are beyond dispute.

Israel caused the closure of the Suez Canal in 1967, burdening the European economy with the consequences. In the war now taking place, it has hit the exporting ports in the eastern Mediterranean, burdening Europe with another cut in its supplies.

For the third time there is a war resulting from Israel's defiance of our legitimate rights with the backing and support of the United States. This prompts the Arabs to adopt a decision not to continue to make economic sacrifices by producing quantities of their vital oil wealth in excess of what is justified by the economic factors in their states unless the world community moves to put matters in order, compel Israel to withdraw from our occupied lands, and make the United States aware of the exorbitant price the great industrial states are paying as a result of its blind and unbounded support for Israel.

Therefore, the Arab Oil Ministers meeting on 17 October in the city of Kuwait have decided immediately to begin reducing production in every Arab oil producing country by no less than five per cent of the production for the month of September. The same procedure will be applied every month and production will be reduced by the same percentage of the previous month's production until the Israeli forces are completely evacuated from all the Arab territories occupied in the June 1967 war and the legitimate rights of the Palestinian people are restored.

The conferees are eager that this production should not affect any friendly state which has helped or will help the Arabs in a fruitful and effective manner. They will continue to be supplied with oil in the same quantities which they used to obtain before the reduction. The same special treatment will be given to every state which adopts an important measure against Israel to persuade it to end its occupation of the usurped Arab territories.

The Arab Ministers appeal to all peoples of the world, most of all the American people, to support the Arab nation in its struggle against Israeli colonialism and occupation. They emphasize the sincere desire of the Arab nation to cooperate fully with the peoples of the world, and the Arab nation's readiness to supply the world with oil despite all sacrifices when the world shows sympathy towards us and condemns the aggression against us.

SWB, ME/4428/A/1 – 2

100   Statement of the Ministerial Council of OAPEC, Kuwait, 5 November 1973

The Arab Oil Ministers met in Kuwait for the second time, on 4 and 5 November 1973 and studied the way their first decision had been implemented and its results. They have made decisions, including:

1   The total reduction of production by every Arab state which implemented the decision shall be 25 per cent of the production of the month of September, including the quantities deducted as a result of cutting off supplies to the United States and the Dutch market. After that the reduction will continue in December by five per cent of the November production. The reduction will not affect the share which every friendly state has been importing from each Arab oil exporting country during the first nine months of the current year.

2   The Algerian Energy Minister and the Saudi Oil Minister shall be sent to the Western capitals to explain the Arab viewpoint regarding the oil decisions made at the two meetings held by the Arab Oil Ministers.

SWB, ME/4443/4 – 5

101   Decisions of the XXXVI Meeting of the OPEC Conference, 19 – 20 November 1973

The Conference examined the structure and determination of petroleum prices. To this end the Conference decided that the Economic Commission meet four times a year and that the first of such meetings should be held on Monday, 17 December 1973, in Vienna.

The Conference noted the communiqué issued by the oil companies following the meeting of their representatives with OPEC ministers at OPEC Headquarters on Saturday, 17 November, 1973. The Conference wishes to reiterate that this meeting took place at the request of the companies and it was expected that they would submit to the Conference a constructive proposal. Instead, the companies' representatives dwelt vaguely on ideas for pricing petroleum on the basis of a rigid and arbitarily predetermined procedure divorced from normal market forces. The Conference is not in agreement with such an approach and believes that the pricing of petroleum, like the pricing of other internationally traded manufactured goods, commodities and raw materials, should be market-oriented.

OPEC Press Release, 20 November 1973

102   Decisions of the Ministerial Meeting of the Six Gulf Member Countries of OPEC, 22 – 23 December 1973

The Ministers of the six Gulf Member Countries met in Tehran on 22 and 23 December 1973. The meeting was also attended by other OPEC Delegations, Algeria, Indonesia, Libya and Nigeria, and Venezuela as an observer.

The Ministers reviewed the report prepared by the Economic Commission Board held in Vienna between 17 and 20 December 1973.

Although the findings of the Economic Commission Board, as well as direct sales realized by some of the Member Countries, indicated a price in excess of Dollars 17 per barrel, the Ministerial Committee decided to set government-take of Dollars 7 per barrel for the marker crude, Arabian Light 34 degree API. The relevant posted price for this crude will, therefore, be Dollars 11.651 per barrel. The effective date for this posted price shall be 1 January, 1974. This posted price has already taken into consideration the effect of Geneva II Agreement.

It was also decided to hold an Extraordinary Meeting of the Conference on 7 January, 1974, to discuss the bases of a long-term pricing policy and to review the possibility of establishing a dialogue between oil producing and consuming countries in order to avoid entering into a spiral increase in prices and to protect the real value of their oil.

Considering that the government-take of Dollars 7 per barrel is moderate, the Ministers hope that the consuming countries will refrain from further increase of their export prices.

OPEC Press Release, 24 December 1973

Reading List

There is an enormous literature on the Middle East, much of it strongly partisan. The following list offers a guide to further reading, especially to the memoir material.

Memoirs, etc.
M. Begin, *The Revolt*, London, 1952, new ed. 1979.
D. Ben-Gurion, *Recollections*, London, 1970.
D. Ben-Gurion, *Letters to Paula*, London, 1971.
N. & H. Bentwich, *Mandate Memories, 1918 – 1948*, London 1965.
M. Dayan, *Story of My Life*, London, 1976.
A. Eban, *An Autobiography*, London, 1977.
A. Eban, *Voice of Israel*, London, 1958.
J. Glubb, *A Soldier with the Arabs*, London, 1957.
M. Heikal, *The Road to Ramadan*, London, 1975.
Y. Herzog, *A People that Dwells Alone*, London, 1975.
S. Lloyd, *Suez 1956*, London, 1978.
J.G. McDonald, *My Mission in Israel 1948 – 1951*, London 1951.
G. Meir, *My Life*, London, 1975.
A. Nutting, *No End of a Lesson: The Story of Suez*, London, 1967.
A. al-Sadat, *In Search of Identity*, London 1978.
C. Weizmann, *Trial and Error*, London, 1949.

Secondary works
G. Antonius, *The Arab Awakening*, London 1938.
H. Cattan, *Palestine: The Arabs and Israel*, London, 1969.
M.J. Cohen, *Palestine: Retreat from the Mandate*, London, 1978.
I. Friedman, *The Question of Palestine 1914 – 1918*, London 1973.
W.K. Kazziha, *Palestine in the Arab Dilemma*, London, 1979.
E. Kedourie, *England and the Middle East*, London, 1956.
W. Laqueur, *The Road to War 1967*, London 1968.
W. Laqueur, *Confrontation*, London, 1974.

P. Mangold, *Superpower Intervention in the Middle East*, London, 1977.

P. Mansfield, *Nasser's Egypt*, London, 1969.

P. Mansfield, *The Arabs*, rev. ed. London 1978.

J. Marlowe, *The Seat of Pilate*, London, 1959.

E. Monroe, *Britain's Moment in the Middle East*, London, 1963.

W.B. Quandt, *Decade of Decisions: American Policy towards the Arab-Israeli Conflict 1967 – 1976*, Berkeley, London, 1978.

L. Stein, *The Balfour Declaration*, London 1961.

R. Stephens, *Nasser*, London, 1971.

H. Thomas, *The Suez Affair*, London 1966.

C. Sykes, *Cross Roads to Israel*, London 1965.

A.L. Tibawi, *A Modern History of Syria including Lebanon and Palestine*, London 1969.

P.J. Vatikiotis, *The Modern History of Egypt*, London, 1969.

A. Williams, *Britain and France in the Middle East and North Africa*, London 1968.

Index

Index